Praise for *The Little Black Apron*

"*The Little Black Apron* is a testament that eating healthfully can be quick and easy as well as delicious. A great read for any woman in her twenties and thirties juggling a busy life and also wanting to develop good eating habits."

—**Lisa R. Young,** PhD, RD, author, *The Portion Teller Plan: The No-Diet Reality Guide to Eating, Cheating, and Losing Weight Permanently*, and adjunct assistant professor, New York University

"I don't know how I've survived all of these years without *The Little Black Apron*; no woman's cupboard is complete without one! *The Little Black Apron* is sure to revolutionize the culinary skills of every single, single woman: one apron at a time. Now I finally know the difference between sieve and sear, bravo!"

—**Taryn Winter Brill**, anchor, CBS-TV/CW stations

"The ladies behind *The Little Black Apron* have managed to sneak a bounty of critical information into the pages of this sassy little narrative of a single girl's life. Reading between the lines of entertaining and oh-so-honest commentary, the sexy single gal will definitely learn a thing or two about her body, her health, and even her kitchen!"

—**Amanda Schull**, actress and dancer

"*The Little Black Apron* is a spirited guide to making you feel as comfortable in your kitchen as you are in your ballet flats. Every savvy single should have one on her bookshelf."

—**Ellie Krieger**, TV chef, host of Food Network's *Healthy Appetite*, and author of *Small Changes, Big Results*

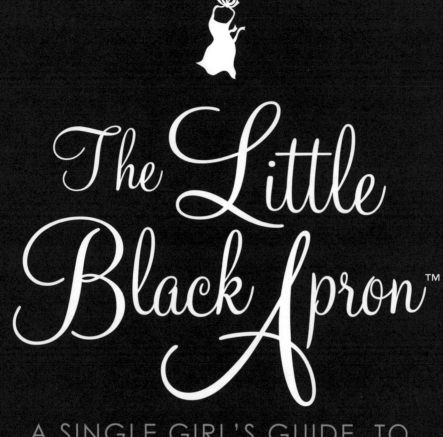

The Little Black Apron™

A SINGLE GIRL'S GUIDE TO COOKING WITH STYLE & GRACE

JODI CITRIN, M.S., R.D. , MELISSA GIBSON & KATIE NUANES

POLKA DOT press®

Avon, Massachusetts

for our grandmothers

Published by Polka Dot Press
An imprint of Adams Media,
an F+W Publications Company
57 Littlefield Street
Avon, MA 02322
www.adamsmedia.com

ISBN-10: 1-59869-206-2
ISBN-13: 978-1-59869-206-8

Printed in Canada.

J I H G F E D C B A

This book is available at quantity discounts for bulk purchases. For information, please call 1-800-289-0963.

Library of Congress Cataloging-in-Publication Data
Citrin, Jodi.
The little black apron / Jodi Citrin, Melissa Gibson, and Katie Nuanes.
p.   cm.
ISBN-13: 978-1-59869-206-8 (pbk.)
ISBN-10: 1-59869-206-2 (pbk.)
1. Cookery. I. Gibson, Melissa. II. Nuanes, Katie.
III. Title.
TX714.C497 2007
641.5—dc22
2007018899

Contents

salads

veggies and sides

chicken, pork, beef, seafood, and frittatas

starches and pastas

desserts

beverages

vinaigrettes,
sauces, and
marinades

acknowledgments

We'd like to express our warmest gratitude to our dearest friends (and fellow single girls) in New York, San Francisco, Los Angeles, Orange County, Chicago, Denver, and Honolulu for encouraging us to charge forward with our oh-so-brilliant idea of cooking-for-one. You are each our inspiration and we can't thank you enough for the memories, the laughter, the hangovers, the years of friendship and those to come.

We certainly wouldn't have had the opportunity to save domestic newbies, one kitchen utensil at a time, if it hadn't been for the incredible faith of our agent, Carol Mann—our sincerest thanks.

And our enormous thanks to our editor, Jennifer Kushnier, for her delightful wit, constant encouragement, and hilarious edits that had us laughing out loud—four-letter words and all.

But most of all, much love and thanks to our parents—Niles and Nancy Citrin, Michael and Lisa Gibson, and Mike and Mary Nuanes—and families who span oceans and continents, for their love, constant support, and belief in each of us.

foreword

Cooking is lifelong journey that cannot commence without the basics. Once these fundamental skills are tested and refined, cooking can transcend into a passionate and fulfilling experience throughout a lifetime. Instilling this passion in others is what the authors of *The Little Black Apron*—Jodi Citrin, Katie Nuanes, and Melissa Gibson— embody throughout their book. Learning to cook for one's self ignites the timeless habits of nutrition, wellness, and a love for flavor.

From their hilarious vignettes about life, to their nutritional guidelines for healthy living, to the abundant, yet simple recipes-for-one, Jodi, Melissa, and Katie are an inspiration to the next generation of cooks. In my experience, you don't have to be a trained chef to appreciate the robustness of seasonal produce and high-quality ingredients. Each recipe in *The Little Black Apron* incorporates these simple pleasures of life and yet is approachable. *The Little Black Apron* speaks with an authentic voice that resonates with its generation—women who have avoided the kitchen their entire lives—peer to peer.

When teaching others how to cook in my kitchen, I always stress quality, flavor, and simplicity. Jodi, Melissa, and Katie stress these basic principles with humor and grace while discussing not only their adventures in life, but also their relationship with food. It's this fundamental approach to food and life that guides the reader through each recipe and chapter with a smile on her face.

Annie Somerville, Chef
Greens Restaurant
San Francisco, CA

the little black apron
the must-have tool for every newbie chefette

We're betting that, for the first time since high school, you've been waking up at 7 A.M. (Unless, of course, you're one of the fortunate few who decided to work market hours, in which case, you get extra super sympathy for keeping capitalism alive and well. We thank you.)

We'd also wager, based on our own experiences, that the last thing you're thinking about when you wake is what you're doing for dinner twelve hours later.

Chances are that between the time you embark on your journey to work, put in a full day, and commute home, the thought of cooking dinner for one person (AKA *you*) is beyond your scope of daily torture. Now, this is not to say that you wouldn't love to have a home-cooked meal to devour each evening, but who has the time, much less the wherewithal to do so? Keep reading and you'll see. It *is* possible for you to create savory home-cooked meals in your bachelorette years.

We know you exist because we've been exactly where you are. (Yes, even Katie didn't know how to navigate a kitchen, back in the days when she carried aerosol hairspray in her purse for emergency puffy-bang re-puffing purposes.) You're a single girl who doesn't know a can opener from a whisk. Deep down inside, however, you have dreams of living the domestic life and being an amazing mother and wife while residing in your newly remodeled Connecticut farmhouse. And, although you have never admitted this openly, you already neurotically contemplate the day when you won't be able to fix your three-year-old child a grilled-cheese sandwich. Nor will you be able to serve egg-salad sandwiches for "ladies' luncheons" because you don't know how to make a decent hard-boiled egg (given that all attempts to date have ended with putrid green yolks).

Moreover, you are so completely embarrassed about not knowing how to cook or entertain that you continue to order takeout each night and suggest restaurant gatherings when entertaining friends. In your attempt to overcome your lack of domestic prowess, you purchase *Living* even though you don't understand half the terms or ingredients Martha calls for in the recipes. How can you *not* know what haricots, Gruyère, or turmeric are when you have an interdisciplinary degree in economics and political science?

At least, that's how *we've* felt during our grueling, post-college years. Below is a snapshot of our typical day. If the following sliver of our reality mirrors even slightly what you feel on a periodic basis, then this book was written for you. Frighteningly, our post-teenage years have skipped along the same path for an unmentionable duration of time (let's just say we're well into our high-school reunions):

8:00 A.M.

The chilling realization that the morning commute—in an archaic hand-me-down clunker of a car inherited back when gas was $0.99 per gallon and the Kyoto Conference was still being attended by the United States—is slowly, tank by tank, consuming what we once thought would become a nest egg. Or, as the occasional mass-transit darlings, we've been assaulted by lethal body odor permeating from the "gentleman" seated much too close or propositioned by the toothless ticket attendant, and we've endured stifling heat as a result of the 150-plus bodies crammed in a single subway car. Overall, though, we took comfort (albeit slight) in the fact that we'd be able to pay our gas bills and/or monthly public transportation passes by spending the next eight to ten hours slaving away for "The Man" in our cushy cubicles.

9:00 A.M.–5:00 P.M.

First and foremost, congratulate yourself on being employed. No matter how many careers we've amassed between us, we've learned one thing: Paychecks are incredible. They are one of the most influential change agents to the female professional's perspective on life. All those years in high school and college classes preparing to enter the work force have not only made us appreciate how difficult working can be, but more important, how liberating and empowering income is to our sense of self. What having a job did not inspire us to consider, however, was cooking dinner for ourselves. How could it, when we couldn't even make a decision about what to eat for lunch from the corner deli?

5:00 P.M.–6:00 P.M.

It is only after we'd dislodge ourselves from our ergonomically advanced office chairs at the end of our day that we'd remember two things:

1. We have to commute home.
2. We should probably "work out" in the hope that our now not-so-firm bottoms will miraculously defy both Darwinism and gravity after a short stint on the treadmill/bike/elliptical. If you spin . . . much mazel tov.

6:00 P.M.–7:00 P.M.

If only to postpone the commute, we'd drag ourselves to the local meat market—the gym, that is, not the grocery store—for some pathetically short duration of time (approximately half an hour). On days that we'd break a sweat or experience a shortness of breath, we'd immediately thrilled and decide to take the next day off. That being said, why is it always that the girl on the treadmill next to you looks like she's been running for three days straight sans food and water? Despite the fact that she is perhaps living your personal hell, she's basically worked out for the both of you, so why bother?

7:00 P.M.–8:00 P.M.

We'd finally stumble back into our 400-square-foot apartment and truly lack the energy, despite finding inner chi only thirty minutes prior in yoga, to muster the gumption to make dinner. What's more depressing than the inevitable inhalation of yet another pizza for dinner is that "home" is smaller than a freshman dorm room and costs more than half your *take-home income.*

Let's pause here for a second to talk about the concept of take-home income. Okay, if you had a similar reaction to the mysteries of your first paycheck that we did, you are dumbfounded. Truly perplexed. We understand the importance of Social Security, federal taxes, state taxes, health care, blah blah blah, but it honestly takes everything—literally everything—in us not to calculate on a bimonthly basis (the first and the fifteenth) approximately how many pairs of *shoes* (fill in your own personal accessory weakness; purses and jewelry are other favorites of ours) those withholdings equate to annually. Oh, wait, we mean how much we could additionally contribute to our 401(k)s and Roth IRAs. (Sorry, Moms. We just had a temporary lapse in our fiduciary responsibilities.) Shoes. It's always the shoes. Your mother has openly admitted that she's failed at raising you to become a productive beancounter. Instead of unwrapping new pairs of shoes or handbags at Christmas or Hanukkah, you're opening books titled *Female Fiscal Responsibility, Girl Power and Money, Understanding Your Personal Finances,* and *Don't Spend Any More Money on Shoes or Handbags.*

But back to why the working girl doesn't cook dinner for herself each and every night. For starters, she never imagined she'd have this obscene level of responsibility. We're just going to put it out there and state the obvious: *Working is much more difficult than going to school.* No one—specifically Mom and Dad—ever disclosed this priceless gem of information. Why? *Because they didn't want to pay for a collegiate experience any longer.* Somehow the memo "Advantages of Staying in School Forever: Why

getting a JD/MBA, a PhD in philosophy, and an MA in art history with a concentration in sixteenth-century Flemish ceramics is more advantageous than *working*" was misplaced.

So you've been cut off from the mother ship, and life-impacting decisions no longer have anything to do with selecting classes that begin only after 11 A.M. and don't meet on Fridays. Nowadays, as opposed to having massive anxiety attacks over not getting into the same psychology class with your two best friends (so you can compare crossword puzzle answers during lecture), you're losing sleep over how to choose your health care policy: PPO versus HMO; how to pay for gas, cable, electricity, a cell phone, and your student loans; and how to wake up in the morning and schlep to the same place and do the same thing, each and every single day. You are seriously considering throwing in the towel and moving home with your parents. As much as you might want to hurl yourself over a cliff at the mere thought, the prospect of having a meal waiting for you on the table when you get home from work is seductive. *Do not make this asinine mistake.*

We're here to placate a few of your seemingly insurmountable fears surrounding your lack of culinary aptitude. In the following chapters, we will help you through the roughest patches of your week—that is, Sunday through Thursday. We've outlined the very basics of how to create nutritious meals for one that take around thirty minutes to cook and actually have taste. You might not know what miso or orecchiette are or what to do with them, but your taste buds will thank you. Our veggies, salads, sides, proteins, starches, and desserts not only satiate the ever-so-sensitive and demanding palette, but they're geared toward helping you implement a more nutritious diet. Not only will you feel better when you're eating nutritiously, but over time it will aid in the "shock and awe" combat against your ass on its quest to spread beyond the limits of your skirt seam. (Trust us on this one.) Hopefully, learning to cook for yourself will help you save a little extra cashola for new shoes—or your 401(k).

For the record, we always went for the shoes, so don't sweat the guilt.

Miss Piggy

"Never eat more than you can lift."

CHAPTER ONE

grocery shopping
for the single girl

If your Sunday shopping experience is anything like ours were until we embraced the Zen of the grocery store, it goes something like this . . .

At some point on Sunday afternoon, you work up the energy to trek down to Safeway (AKA DateWay), Whole Foods (AKA Whole PayCheck), or Trader Joe's (the greatest shopping experience *ever*). You grab the corroded and most certainly unsanitary shopping cart outside and head toward the produce section. Yes, that's the first section in most supermarkets, the one with all the *fresh* fruit and vegetables. Keep on truckin', you're doing fine. Everything's going smoothly, you're under control, and then out of nowhere, the manic shopper in you takes hold of all decision-making skills you had only moments before.

You suddenly think that buying eight zucchinis, two gargantuan heads of broccoli, and seventeen Brussels sprouts (not that you really even know what they are, but they are just precious looking . . . and you're a sucker for miniature cabbages) and whipping them into an impromptu veggilicious concoction is a burst of culinary genius. An hour later, you return to your kitchen with said veggilicious concoction ingredients, plus a few more "bargain buys": three apples, seven pears (they're both on sale for $1.99 a pound), a bunch of bananas (always need bananas), a few red peppers (it's always

pepper season), five pounds of ground chuck ($2.49 a pound . . . so hey, why not load up, it's a bargain), three blocks of Tillamook Cheddar (Cheddar makes everything better), the incredible edible eggs, a package of fifty corn tortillas (again on sale), and let's not forget dessert, the most important part of the meal.

Three weeks pass, and early one Monday morning you saunter into your kitchen to prepare your daily dose of personal bliss (coffee) when you're abruptly interrupted by an insidious stench emanating from the refrigerator. Luckily you have your wits about you and escape the room with only moments to spare. Thank God you religiously watched *Reno 911* and know what do to in an emergency—asphyxiation from rotting refrigerator enigmas would not be the most heroic way of departing this life.

There is a feng shui method to follow while grocery shopping. We live by a few Zen-enabling parameters that will guide your shopping experience. While we can't prevent rotting refrigerator enigmas, we can promise that by embodying the tips (on the facing page), you'll eventually become a cognoscente of what types of food you are buying and how much you should buy.

how not to become the manic grocery shopper

- Always shop on a full stomach, not when you are hungry. When you're hungry, everything looks good. That tiny box of Cheddar crackers shaped like elephant ears that cost more than a good sushi meal is too tempting to resist. And these crackers will sit indefinitely in your cabinet because you feel too guilty to throw them away.

- Make a list, including how many of each item you need, before you go to the store to prevent impulsive buys. And don't buy anything not on the list.

- Shop primarily around the perimeter of the store, where all the fresh and healthy products are—fruits, vegetables, meat, and dairy. The middle aisles contain the packaged foods that have a long shelf-life, such as cookies, candy, chips, and soda.

- When you do venture down these middle aisles, look on the high and low shelves. The foods at eye level tend to be the least healthy options.

- Beware of the word *reduced*, such as "reduced-fat" peanut butter/chocolate swirl/chocolate ice cream. Reduced fat is not synonymous with healthy, nor is it synonymous with low-fat or low-calorie.

- If it sounds too good to be true, such as "zero" calories, it probably is.

- Ingredient lists should have more recognizable words than not.

- Avoid the candy bar temptation while you stand in line. If that Kit Kat is calling your name, distract yourself by picking up a gossip magazine. While the Kit Kat may seem like a great idea at that moment, an extra half-hour at the gym later will make you regret it.

Size Does Matter

We live in an increasingly size-conscious society. More often than not, we're conditioned to believe that bigger is better. Unfortunately, bigger people are *not* considered "better." Whether this is primarily indicative of American culture or of a global trend among developing nations, it's hard to say, but we are inundated by countless impressions of our *growing* society. Bigger people lead to bigger houses lead to bigger cars lead to bigger parking places lead to bigger mega-malls lead to bigger shopping carts lead to bigger produce and packaged goods lead to bigger meals lead to bigger people. A vicious cycle, indeed.

It's hard to miss the growing obesity problem in our country. Whether you've witnessed it in the airport lounge (desperately hoping that your window seat isn't next to *that* person's seat), watched it on the *Today* show, or participated in it by super-sizing your French fries, chances are that you, consciously or unconsciously, are partaking in this social trend of Bigger is Better.

Increased portion size is often to blame for this obesity epidemic. Despite the ubiquitous use of the term, most people do not know how to quantify a portion. The reason for this lack of knowledge is that portion measurements have been changing over the last few decades, much like the actual size of a "size six" little black dress. Packaged foods are bigger than they were ten, twenty, and thirty years ago. Recipes yield fewer servings than they once did as portion sizes have increased. Plates and cups are also manufactured to be larger. What was considered a "large" in the 1970s is now considered a "small" at most fast-food chains.

What does this mean for you? It means that the average individual is eating more food. Chances are, you are one of those individuals. Numerous studies have shown that the more food we're served, the more we'll eat. As a result, our ability to recognize our body's "fullness" has been dulled and we're unable to gauge our sense of satisfaction. Many of us have lost the ability to know when we are *actually* hungry. And if we don't know when we're hungry, we can't read our bodies' clues telling us when to stop eating.

Now you're just hoping your most recent "growth spurt" will end soon, as you're about to bust through your new pair of True Religion jeans and you can't afford another pair. Thoughts of plunging deep into the red over a pair of jeans (which cost as much as most people spend on their monthly car payment) is motivation enough for you to understand portion sizes. Your inability to measure a serving of pasta is chipping away at your retirement, given the number of jeans you bought last year alone. So, what can you do? Watch portion sizes.

We are so accustomed to large portions that we don't even realize how much we're eating. But have no fear. There are tricks to help you eat less while still feeling satisfied. When you sit down to eat, you actually determine how full you're going to be before you even touch the food. That's because you decide, visually, whether it seems like enough to fill you up. So, to feel like you're eating more, switch to smaller plates and bowls. Food will fill up the smaller plate or bowl so you'll automatically feel like you're eating more. This will bring you one step closer to managing portion sizes.

A Portion Does *Not* Constitute Whatever Fits on a Plate or in a Glass

Portion sizes are small. Repeat: Portion sizes are small. If you need to take an emotional breather for what we're about to discuss, you might want to make yourself a pedi-mani appointment or renew your subscription to *US Weekly*, as you're going to need the pick-me-up. We present this concept to prepare you for what you will read in the chart

A Few Simple Portion Size Conversions

*3 ounces meat, fish, poultry =
a deck of cards or the palm of your hand*

1 ounce cheese = 4 small dice

1 ounce pretzels = fistful

½ cup cooked rice = ice cream scoop

1 teaspoon oil or butter = tip of a thumb

2 tablespoons peanut butter = Ping-Pong ball

1 cup cold cereal = baseball

*½ cup ice cream = ½ baseball (beware of this
one—this is the serving size listed on most ice
cream containers and it's very small)*

1 baked potato = closed fist

6 ounces liquid = teacup

above. This is not to say that you can't have two or even three servings of a particular food. However, if you are having ten times a serving size, be alarmed. That bottomless bowl of pasta is not going to help you fit into your jeans on Friday night. And it has nothing to do with the carbs and everything to do with the fact that you just ate three days' worth of pasta in one sitting.

Carol Siskind

"I can't cook.
I use a smoke alarm as a timer."

CHAPTER TWO

the basics
learning to love your kitchen

Admitting that you have a fear is the first step in overcoming it. Identifying why you are intimidated by your kitchen is critical to expanding your culinary confidence.

It kills you to admit that you know nothing about basic kitchen vernacular: the difference between baking and broiling, how to differentiate between dry and liquid measuring cups, how to distinguish cumin from curry, and how to dice an onion. Every time you're asked to defrost anything but a TV dinner, you become so overwhelmed and nervous that you exude a pungent perspiration resembling cat urine. You think your friends have begun to notice.

While you might want to consider obtaining prescription deodorant, neither cooking nor your fear of your kitchen are worth losing friends over. Chin up; you have conquered more sensitive and complex battles before in your life. *Confidence and perspective are the crux of learning to cook. Confidence is increased by accruing experience. Perspective is increased by reflecting upon those experiences.* While there are many examples that illustrate this journey of building confidence and perspective (learning French, riding a bike, and avoiding awkward second dates with men your best friend's mother set you up with), there is one particular activity that exemplifies this process of growing from awkward to skilled: sex.

Think back upon your anxiety-ridden adolescence and about how you would get through your "first time." The hours you spent imagining what it would be like, who it would be with, and perhaps most importantly, whether it would be good. It's that last question that's the most perplexing. No doubt, you feel that with each subsequent performance you learned something. Regardless of it being good, bad, or ugly (the sex, not the guy . . . we hope), your breadth of knowledge has been expanded. You discover a new technique, a new term, or perhaps a new accessory. Reflecting upon where you started in your sexual career and where you are today, you realize how your confidence has blossomed. (And if it hasn't, you're doing something wrong . . . which is the topic for another book.)

Your kitchen is the next room you are destined to surmount. Just as your sexual confidence steadily grew with time and practice, so will your finesse with cooking. (And, much as in the bedroom, sporting a seductive getup helps you get in the mood. In this case, we recommend, naturally, a little black apron.) By cultivating a robust culinary vocabulary, developing your understanding of the utensils used in various recipes, and dedicating yourself to experimenting in your kitchen, regardless of failure, you will become a better and certainly a confident chef. Each recipe you try will grow your confidence, and with time you'll notice that your inner chef has a signature style of her own. So be bold! And remember: Whenever your culinary confidence begins to wane, think back upon all of "the firsts" in your life and how far you've come.

Culinary Vocabulary

Before we launch into the remaining chapters, we're going to come clean about the cooking vernacular and lay it out sur la table. Despite many of the following terms having French etymological roots, they're not sexy. They're not glamorous. And they have absolutely nothing to do with haute couture. We have no desire to torture you with banal and obvious definitions. However, we are confident that the following refresher course will increase your culinary confidence. By embracing the nomenclature of the average epicure, you'll be as well versed as M.F.K. Fisher and Julia Child—two of the most influential epicures of the past century.

Al dente: You've heard this phrase countless times. While you feign knowing the meaning of this term, you still have *no* idea. So impress the waiter the next time you order linguini with clam sauce and ask for it *al dente*. Its literal translation in Italian means "to the tooth." Pasta should be cooked well enough, but still have a wee resistance in the middle when bitten.

Bake: This verb is located on the knob of your oven for a reason. It rhymes with *fake*. Used in a sentence: "Prior to my departure for a tropical spring *break*, I like to *fake* and *bake*." *Baking* food in your oven is similar. The technique is one that naturally causes food to slowly evaporate moisture with heat which thus concentrates the flavor. When in doubt, the most common temperature for baking is 350°F.

Baste: In juxtaposition to baking, basting aids in the prevention of drying. Think suntan oil. Think laying out on the beach and missing that spot right under your armpit. Basting means that you coat roasting meat in liquid fat (olive oil, canola oil, etc.) or in its own fat, AKA pan drippings. You'll both prevent it from drying out and maintain the highest level of flavor. Basting tools include a brush, spoon, or baster. With this knowledge, you'll be prepared when you tackle the Thanksgiving turkey.

Beat: You're driving along, listening to Mozart or *The Sound of Music* soundtrack. Suddenly the flamingo-pink jalopy in the right lane swerves abruptly, forcing you to nearly crash into the brand spanking new SLK 500 on your left. You want to *beat* the derelict driver to a pulp. It's the same for cooking. Using a spoon, fork, or **whisk**, you rapidly **whip**, or stir, the ingredients you're mixing. (Blenders and mixers also can be used if you are averse to kitchen calisthenics.)

Bind: If you've ever been to a dull cocktail party, you've been tempted to thicken the conversation with an outrageous comment. By adding a juicy tidbit of gossip, you'd survive the pathetic banter that is encouraging the onset of a numbing migraine. Butter, cream, eggs, and flour are used in a similar manner to thicken sauces when you add and stir them into the liquid over heat. *Binding* not only refers to thickening, but also something that holds a mixture together. For instance, eggs are the *binder* in meatloaf.

Blacken: Film noir could easily be likened to this ubiquitous Cajun-style cooking method. It fires you up. It titillates your palate. It leaves you charred, but wanting more. *Blackening* occurs when seasoned foods are quickly cooked in a sizzling skillet, creating a singed texture.

Blanch: Visions of Blanche DuBois and Stanley Kowalski dance in your head. But alas, this verb has nothing to do with *A Streetcar Named Desire*, unless Tennessee Williams was working on some serious double entendres. To *blanch*, as one would a fruit or vegetable, requires one to bring water to a boil, boil the desired fruit or vegetable to the desired doneness (about 30 seconds), and then immediately plunge it into ice water (to prevent it from cooking further). Many times *blanching* is used to aid in the peeling of skin from the fruit or vegetable. *Blanching* maintains firmness and taste, such that not *all* crispness, color, and flavor are obliterated. Your grandmother's method of cooking broccoli, which resulted in brownish green-tinted mush, should encourage you to blanch your vegetables more often than not.

Blend: Blended families. Blended homes. Blended races. Blended cultures. One can only hope the world will become a peaceful playground of blended methodologies and ideologies. Can anyone say McDonald's in Milwaukee, Tokyo, Moscow, and New Delhi? To *blend* in your kitchen is to mix two or more ingredients together, resulting in equal distribution.

Boil: Get a pot. Fill it with water. Place it on your stovetop. Turn the burner on high. Watch and wait. Water begins to bubble and rumble. Now, you have *boiled*. The *boiling* stage for water occurs at 212°F.

Braise: There's a reason we tend to find ourselves engrossed by trashy tabloid magazines and pedestrian talk shows—they're juicy. This cooking technique requires browning meat in juicy oils, fats, or other liquids. Once the meat has been browned it is slowly cooked submerged about three-quarters, which results in the breakdown of fats and connective tissues while maintaining its juices, thus making it tender to bite.

Bread: This technique, for some strange reason, just makes everything taste delicious. Perhaps it's the carbs. Perhaps it's the extra calories. All we know is that *breading* makes it better. *Breading* requires you to coat the food with bread crumbs. Many times you have to cover the food in beaten eggs or another **binding** liquid in order to moisten the food enough for the bread crumbs to stick. Don't forget to shake off excess crumbs, which can burn while cooking.

Broil: If you've ever spent more than thirty minutes reading skin-care pamphlets in your dermatologist's lobby, then you have some concept of the verb *broil*. The sun will *broil* your complexion. This is also how you *broil* food, by placing it *under* a direct heat source. Using the broiler in your oven is great for things like fish (which requires a quick cooking time), developing a golden crust on things like mac and cheese, or even just making toast.

Broth: The flavored liquid resulting from cooking meat, vegetables, or fish in water. It is often used interchangeably with **stock** and *bouillon*.

Brown: A method that we like to associate with Mystic Tan. Much like a raw piece of meat, you find yourself in a suffocating area being sprayed with a mysterious liquid that enhances your appeal. *Browning* mimics this process: a speedy **sautéing**, **broiling**, or **grilling** in butter, oil, or liquid that increases flavor, texture, and/or eye appeal.

Brush: Chances are you've sported a pedicure or two in your time. Though you'll readily admit you've forgotten how to paint your own toes, you're well aware that a brush is being used to paint your nails. Two or three coats of Ballet Slipper or Edinburgh and your Saturday routine has begun. We're hoping you're willing and able to use a **pastry brush** to coat a food with liquids such as melted butter, olive oil, sugar glaze, etc. because it's the easiest way to sparingly add flavor without dousing something in a calorie-rich sauce.

Caramelize: This refers to the process of cooking sugars until they have browned, whether done on the stovetop, in the oven, or on a **grill**, imparting a richer flavor and visually pleasing color. *Caramelizing* can be used for fruits, vegetables, fish, meats, or poultry, where the surface of the food that has made direct contact with heat develops a brown crust. Many times *caramelizing* is done to onions or shallots with sugar.

Chop: Karate chop. Chop suey. Chop shop. Chopper. You're getting the idea. This cooking term requires you to cut food into irregular but relatively equal-sized shaped pieces. Think of creating pieces no wider than the size of a penny.

Cream: While the legendary group of rock 'n' roll or the epic song that defined the 1980s have nothing to do with this technique, we'd bet our slingbacks that both Eric Clapton and Prince have done their fair share of creaming. By **whipping** vegetable shortening, butter, or margarine, with or without sugar, you'll create a light and fluffy mixture that aids in increasing height in cookies and cakes.

Dash: A measure equal to $\frac{1}{16}$ teaspoon, which equals about two pinches of what fits between your pointer finger and thumb.

Dice: What came first: the fuzzy hanging gizmos on rearview mirrors or the culinary term? We don't know. What we do know is that dicing consists of cutting food into very small cubes. Yes, the same geometric shape as the you've-got-to-be-kidding-me dice that typically dangle from Mustangs. A *dice* is technically $\frac{1}{4}" \times \frac{1}{4}"$, or slightly larger than a **mince**.

Fry: Colonel Sanders has created a disturbingly large empire on this method of cooking, much to the dismay of the American Heart Association. While we discourage you from ever engaging in this type of cooking, we'd be deceiving ourselves if we didn't admit that we too relish eating the occasional fritter/hush puppy, popcorn shrimp, and crispy fried chicken. Properly forming the crisp brown crust occurs when the food is submerged in hot cooking oil.

Grate: The expression, "She/he grates on me" sums up the visual we'd like to expound upon. *Grating* cheese, *grating* lemon, *grating* carrots are all accomplished by rubbing the food against a coarse surface (typically a grater) that shreds them into fine pieces. Just think carrot cake, hash browns, and tacos and you'll appreciate *grating*.

Grill: Summer barbecues, the aroma of burning charcoal wafting through the breeze, chilled margaritas, golden tans, sun dresses, and long walks along the ocean. Nostalgia implores us to highlight this term as one of our favorites: a traditional and simple method of cooking foods over a heat source of wood or charcoal in the open air. If you're of the school of thought that considers gas grilling an art form, we forgive you.

Julienne: Perhaps John Lennon was inspired and moved by this method when he named his first child. We understand the difficulty of differentiating between prodigy rock star children's names and this technique, but trust us, once you've cut your first vegetable into long, thin strips (about 2"–3" x ⅟₁₆"–⅛"), you'll understand the power of *julienne*.

Marinate: You've stood next to him in line at the bank. You might have even dated him, briefly. Oh yeah, that guy, the one who marinates in an entire bottle of Stetson before leaving the house. While you might be offended by the overly marinated male, soaking food in aromatic ingredients (teriyaki, barbecue, vinaigrette, garlic and herbs, etc.) increases its flavor tremendously. Things like chicken and other meats can usually be *marinated* overnight, while things like fish and vegetables need a quicker *marinating* time or they'll start to break down from any acids in the marinade before they're cooked.

Mash: This is the method that we're convinced might lend itself to eliminating dimpled cellulite from our thighs. *Mashing* requires one to beat or press food (mmm . . . potatoes . . .), thus removing any lumps and creating a smooth-textured mixture.

Mince: You've often been perplexed by the definition of "mincemeat." You think people eat it. But what is it? The above mentioned is a play on the method by which it's prepared. Mincemeat is a hodgepodge of spices, garlic, vegetables, fruit, and sometimes meat. Thereby, the term *mincing* is **chopping** food items into tiny, irregular pieces. Think: pieces a little smaller than the size of rice grains.

Mix: Mixing and blending are like Siamese twins. If you missed **Blend**, we'll repeat it in mixing terms. Mixed families. Mixed homes. Mixed races. Mixed cultures. One can only hope the world will become a peaceful playground of mixed methodologies and ideologies. Can anyone say McDonald's in Milwaukee, Tokyo, Moscow, and New Delhi? To *mix* in your kitchen is to **blend** two or more ingredients together, which will result in equal distribution.

Pare: In order to curb your spending habits that are whittling away at your retirement, your mother suggested you pare down the number of Christian Louboutins you buy. The same process is used in your kitchen as in your bank account. *Paring* requires trimming and peeling the food, usually fruits and vegetables.

Pinch: Think of some fratastic episode in your past, perhaps in a beer-soaked bar basement, when some charming gentleman decided that pinching your ass was the most strategic way to get you to engage in a mating dance with him. That's the amount we're referring to when we list this measurement: an amount of an ingredient that would fit between your pointer finger and your thumb.

Poach: *Poaching* has come a long way since Medieval times. Serfs, thoroughly perturbed by the baron of their fiefdom, retaliated against him by poaching his deer, pheasants, and various other game and fowl. *Poaching*, as it applies to the modern kitchen, only requires you to gently cook food (pears, chicken, fish, etc.) in liquid (water, mulled brandy with nutmeg, chicken broth, etc.). So much easier, really. *Poaching* occurs between 160°F and 185°F. The liquid is not bubbling, but steam is rising.

Purée: Don't be scared off by the accent aigu; it won't bite you. With years of French grammar school among us, we're convinced that it's only used to bolster the word's confidence and pomp. Therefore, ladies, just think of it as the peacock version of the lackluster method **mash**. See how quickly that deflates its culinary ego. Poof, gone. **Mash** food until it reaches a thick, smooth consistency. The most common way to *purée* is to use a **blender** or **food processor** (pouring the food through a **sieve** can also be done if a finer *purée* is desired)—voilà—le purée.

Reduce/Reduction: It's always fun when a verb stems from a noun or vice versa. Some of our favorite four-letter words were derived from this very same thought process. A *reduction* is the result of the action of *reducing*. It goes something like this: cooking down liquids over a high heat source forces evaporation, thus thickening or intensifying the flavor of a liquid mixture such as a soup or sauce. Whether the liquid is a **stock** (beef, chicken, or vegetable), wine, or another mixture, the decrease in water creates an increase in texture and intensity.

Rib: Now we've all heard the scandal about Janet Jackson having a rib removed to make her waist *appear* narrower. Chances are her plastic surgeon paid close attention in Home Economics. In cooking, the term refers to a "rib" of celery, or a single stalk. Since celery grows in the ground, it is often very dirty once you get it home. An easy way to make sure you get it all off is to wipe it with a damp paper towel.

Roast: A wee history lesson for you Trivial Pursuit buffs. *Roasting* is one of the most ancient methods of cooking (mainly game and fowl) and originally involved a turning spit over fiery coals. Many of the kitchens in castles, manors, and great houses included a spit attached to a treadmill powered by dogs or humans. Fortunately for us, *roasting* only requires one to cook food uncovered in the oven, creating even heat that helps prevent the outside of something burning before the inside has a chance to cook. *Roasting* is great for almost any kind of food . . . meats, fish, vegetables, or fruit.

Rough Chop: This is basically the same as **chop**, except that you cut the food into larger, but still relatively same-sized, pieces.

Sauté: Again, please don't be intimidated by the fluffy French accent. It's a mere distraction in your pursuit of culinary happiness. In fact, chances are you've already mastered this technique. Cooking food with a small pat of butter or oil in a skillet that has been placed over a direct heat source is *sautéing*, voilà!

Sear: Searing is perhaps best described as the cooking "quickie." Much like the five-minute romp, *searing* occurs when food is quickly cooked over extremely hot heat, thus sealing in a meat's juices and creating a golden brown crust.

Shred: If you are a true child of the times, you remember Shredder, the sinister villain from *Teenage Mutant Ninja Turtles*. What this looming assassin did to his prey, you'll do in your kitchen. *Shredding*, either by hand, **food processor**, or **grater**, will tear food into thin, long strips.

Sieve: Rowdy soccer fans sometimes cry "SIEVE!" at a goalie who misses an easy catch, as she let the ball slip right through her arms. Similarly, in order to *sieve* something, inciden-tally, you would use a *sieve* or a strainer, usu-ally with a fine mesh. The purpose in straining a liquid in this manner is to remove any lumps or unwanted larger particles.

Simmer: You're infuriated and you're about to explode. Your ears are burning and a color-ful four-letter word is surfacing to your tongue. You're counting backwards from ten, engaging in breathing exercises, and repeating the man-tra, "Simmer down, simmer down, simmer down." This method of cooking mimics this scenario, by cooking food in a liquid at a low temperature, such that tiny bubbles break the liquid's surface. *Simmering* occurs at between 185°F and 205°F. There are a few bubbles rising and more steam is created than when **poach-ing**, and there are fewer bubbles than when **boiling**. *Simmering* allows foods to cook gently and flavors to combine thoroughly.

Steam: The brownish green-tinted broccoli your grandmother served was a direct result of her misinterpreting the difference between **boil-ing** and *steaming*. Rather than risk loathing vegetables for the balance of your lifetime, you might want to consider this method of prepar-ing food, as it maintains nutrients, shape, and texture. Simply place food on top of a rack (or in a steamer basket) *over* **boiling** water in a covered pan. The food should not be submerged, otherwise you'd have something that is **boiled,** not *steamed*. *Steaming* is great for fish, because it helps keep it moist, and vegetables, because they retain many more nutrients than with **boiling** (unless, of course, you are planning to drink the water the vegetables were boiled in).

Stock: One's potential mate might mention he has good breeding, or come from good *stock*. Here, we mean simply the flavored liquid that is a result of cooking meat, vegetables, or fish in water. It is often used interchangeably with **broth** and *bouillon*.

Toss: You distinctly remember the first time you naively belted out to your friends at a dinner party, "Who wants to give the salad a toss?" Once the raucous laughter died down you were given a lecture on sexual terminology. We'll spare you from revisiting that sermon. The term *tossing* simply means to thoroughly combine several ingredients by mixing lightly.

Vinaigrette: Generally a combination of oil (extra-virgin olive oil is the most common) with vinegar (red wine and balsamic, for example) or acidic juices like lemon. A common proportion is three parts oil to one part vinegar, but we prefer two parts oil to one part vinegar (remember—less oil means less fat). *Vinaigrettes*

are **whisked** together and can be used as salad dressings, marinades, and sauces on anything from meats to vegetables.

Whip: Whip it. Whip it good. Devo was on to something with that gem of a song. Words like **beat** and **cream** and fluffy not only resonate with these lyrics, but strangely enough, with this cooking term. *Whipping*, or vigorously stirring with a spoon, whisk, or electric beater, incorporates air, and as a result, ingredients like eggs or cream transform their physical state into a light and fluffy matter.

Whisk: While you are waiting to be whisked off your feet by some ridiculously stunning (but doesn't know it), sensitive (but not annoyingly metro), kind (but not spineless), hilarious (but doesn't refer to himself as the next Dave Chappelle) man, you might want to utilize this cooking method. **Beating** or fluffing ingredients such as eggs, sugar, vanilla, etc. together with a whisk could be the start of a beautiful relationship. (Warm home-baked cookies, anyone?)

Zest: You've met this person, the one who can only be described as having a lot of gusto. Somehow, you find this grates on your nerves. They exude an overabundance of cheer and it bugs the living shit out of you. However, *zest*, as it relates to cooking, is critical. By **grating** the outer skin of a citrus fruit, you'll shave off the rind, which contains the best oils and pungent flavor of the fruit. The best tool for *zesting* is called a **microplane** (basically just a tiny **grater**) and can be found in many cooking stores.

Utensils: What You Really Need for Your Kitchen

What follows is what we feel is the bare minimum for the bachelorette's kitchen, as you typically don't register at Crate & Barrel until you at least have a fiancé and a wedding date. Sorry to burst your bubble. Now, don't commit hara-kiri just yet, as these are the "must-haves" we think will get you through the next decade—at least until you have a field day registering. And no, none of us has taken that plunge into the depths of the infamous wedding registration mayhem, so we speak the truth.

Now, you might be resistant to adding anything to your arsenal of appliances that currently consists of a toaster that has only one working coil that you inherited your junior year in college. Fear not, the list that follows consists of items that will improve your culinary experience as well as your ability to prepare a well-balanced and nutritious meal. We know it will be difficult to transition from the accessories department to the housewares aisles, but we'll let you in on a little secret. Depending on where you buy these items, they might only amount to the cost of *one* pair of (designer) shoes! And in case you can't decide between a gadget and a Gucci fanny pack, we've listed them in order of highest importance within their groupings.

Spoons and Various Utensils

Spatula (metal and silicon): Perhaps it's the force with which this word "spats" from your lips, but nevertheless, we're in love with both the metal flipping spatula as well as the heat-resistant rubber spatula, which has been tempered to resist high heat while you are cooking. Other rubber spatulas can melt.

Wooden spoons (flat spoon and stirring spoon): Why is it that your mother has fifteen wooden spoons distributed around her kitchen and you have only one? Flat ones work best for pans that have square sides so you can get into those corners. Stirring spoons, well, they stir.

Slotted spoon and pasta spoon: You've always wondered what that "special" spoon was for. Why would a spoon have undulating openings around its edges? Well, now you'll know.

Ladle: (Sing to "Dreidel" tune) Ladle, Ladle, Ladle, it's not made of clay. Ladle, Ladle,

Ladle, use in it your kitchen play. Ladle, Ladle, Ladle, dish it up today. . . .

Garlic press: Trust us; this bad boy is a *must*. Whether it's rubber-handled, metal, or plastic is of no consequence to us. However, the cooking diva's life in the kitchen will never be the same once she's bought her first garlic press. When in the market for a shiny new garlic press of your own, the best way to find a good product is to pick it up and see how it feels to you. It's not rocket science. When in doubt, ask the culinary expert at your local kitchen store which one he or she likes the best.

Peeler: Oh, the peeler. You've most likely been assigned potato peeling duty more than once in your life. Sentenced to a half an hour over the sink or the waste basket while your mother promised you that "you had the best job" of all your siblings and cousins who were also wrangled into preparing part of the *huge* family holiday dinner. Liar. Truth be told, while you might suffer from tormenting Turkey Day flashbacks at first, you'll be thankful you have one in your kitchen. Look for one with a grip handle and a blade that has a knuckle-guard.

Grater: Another pillar of your kitchen. This little piece of culinary genius will save you from ruining your two-day old manicure. No need

to torture your little fingers with mincing and dicing your nails down to their nubs.

Whisk: What else can we say except that we love this utensil? There are obviously a variety of sizes of whisks. Though there are the types of girls who need to have one in every size (mini, small, medium, and large), we'd recommend the midsize whisk to begin your culinary journey.

Tongs: Perhaps one of the most versatile utensils, tongs can be used from your stovetop to the barbecue. That being said, please do *not* confuse kitchen tongs with the outdoor jumbo-sized manly barbecue tongs. While your kitchen tongs can be used on the barbecue, they are typically 12 inches long and are metal—not 2.5 feet long and wooden with metal-edged ends.

Microplane: A microplane is a small, long, thin, one-sided, hand-held grater that produces a very fine grate. Most have a rubber handle at one end for easy maneuvering, and you can even hold it right over your cooking pot and grate the food right into it! Microplanes are perfect for getting the zest off of citrus, grating fresh nutmeg, or even grating hard cheeses like Parmesan. They are readily available at kitchen stores and sometimes even at your local grocery store.

Blender/food processor: Now, while you can easily substitute a blender for a food processor, at some point (when your culinary courage matures), you might want to break down and buy a food processor. In the meantime, the blender you've been using for margaritas since college will do.

Basting/cooking brush: You've always wondered what a paint brush was doing in your mother's kitchen and not in the "arts and crafts" drawer along with the rubber cement and rainbow glitter. Alas, there are many recipes that utilize this most artistic of utensils.

Grill brush: It is very important to clean your grill with the "grill brush" after each use to ensure proper cooking for the next time. (Who was the genius who came up with that name?) You can find this heavy-duty brush at your local home improvement or kitchen store.

Kitchen string: Kitchen string is most often used to hold meats in their shape while roasting. You can buy string from a kitchen store but it's probably cheaper at the hardware store, and it's the same thing. Just consider that savings a little contribution toward your retirement.

Knives

Paring knife: You can use this knife for all sorts of jobs where a chef's knife is too large, as the blade is typically about 3" long. Such utility jobs might include cutting the stem out of a tomato, or even de-veining shrimp.

Chef's knife: Our hope is that you will start thinking of yourself as a fledgling chef and therefore will embrace the knife named after you. Chances are you won't monogram your knives anytime soon, but you will want to use the chef's knife for slicing, dicing, mincing, and chopping. It's a very versatile weapon. Chef's knives come in a variety of lengths so choose what feels most comfortable to you. We like the middle-of-the-road 8-incher.

Steak knife: You've inherited your parents' first silverware set from 1972 and chances are the butter knives are so dull they aren't able to cut boiled carrots. Therefore, we'd highly recommend using a steak knife when you decide you're in the mood for, well, beef, for instance.

Butcher knife: While the three of us grew up across the world from one another, we each have a unifying childhood memory of chasing or being chased around the house by our siblings with a knife—threatening them with death as they'd stolen the remote control and changed the channel preventing us from watching another *Saved by the Bell* rerun. Butcher knives, when not used to torment siblings, are most effective when preparing meats and chopping vegetables.

Serrated knife: Unlike the smooth edge of a chef's knife, a serrated knife has a scalloped edge. It's best for slicing things that are typically hard for a knife to grip, like a tomato. Don't waste your time trying to chop or dice with this knife—it ain't gonna happen. As with the chef's knife, serrated knives are available in an array of lengths so purchase one that feels comfortable to you.

Bread knife: If you haven't used a bread knife or are struggling to determine what type of food its serrated edge is used to cut, perhaps you should e-mail us for a personal culinary consultation. Bread knives are typically at least 12" long, but you can substitute a regular serrated knife.

Steel (knife sharpener): To keep a sharp edge on your knives you should run them along steel after every few uses. Sharpen each side of the blade fifteen times, holding it at a 45-degree angle to the steel.

Pots and Pans

Pots and pans are similar to jewelry or other accessories that are offered in matching sets: It's sometimes best *not* to match. This means that your pots and pans don't all have to be from the same Spring Fantasy Pastel Cookware Collection. While you might be apt to match your pots and pans with the same diligence that you

match your earrings to your necklace to your belt to your shoes to your handbag, this is not a job interview with John Galliano. The materials of which pots and pans are composed—aluminum, stainless steel, cast iron, enamel, and copper—impact the food preparation, thus you should consider having a versatile collection of cookware. The next page has just a few pointers.

7" Sauté pan (with a matching lid): Considered the best match for braising meats or sautéing vegetables, this staple will become your most treasured possession.

10" Skillet: Often considered the granddaddy of all pots and pans, this heavy hitter (literally) will instill the utmost of confidence in your stovetop.

Oven-safe skillet (with a matching lid): An oven-safe skillet can be any size as long as there are no materials on it that could burn, like a plastic handle. We recommend buying a matching lid, and though you won't need it all the time, you'll be elated you have one for the times you do.

1-Quart saucepan (with a matching lid): This little morsel of cookware joy will make you marvel when you are making sauces, sautés, or marinades. Not to mention, it's the smallest one to wash!

switch it up among the following heavy-metal hitters

Aluminum: Consider pots and pans made with aluminum like that favorite pair of jeans that are broken in to the point that you're afraid at any moment you might lose them to your washing machine. Anodized aluminum is always a better bet, as the treatment increases the hardness of the metal, thus distributing heat most evenly. Aluminum cookware is also available in stick-resistant and nonreactive coating, which allows you to cook with more acidic ingredients (wine, vinegar, tomato sauce, etc.) as opposed to those without nonreactive coating, which will incorporate the metallic taste of the aluminum.

Stainless steel: Listen up, ladies, as this will aid in your decision-making: Stainless steel is the only metal that is dishwasher safe. For those of you who still live in an apartment sans a dishwasher (and most likely a disposal), this is a moot point. Stainless steel is often considered best for everyday use; however, select pots that have an aluminum core, as this will distribute the heat more uniformly.

Cast iron: This is going to get a little complicated, so take notes. While cast iron is unparalleled in its searing ability due to its uniform heat conducting character, it shouldn't be used with acidic foods, given their propensity to absorb the metallic taste. While cast iron is intrinsically nonstick for cooking, its cooking surface does have to be properly oiled to prevent rusting. However, enamel-coated cast iron does not require oiling, does not rust, and is perfect for cooking all food types. (Note, however, that enamel is prone to chipping and is not nonstick.)

Copper: Perhaps considered the more refined of the pot and pan materials, copper cookware that is lined with stainless steel or tin is ideal for creating delicate sauces, as it heats and cools very quickly. In line with this delicate nature, they tend to tarnish quickly and therefore must be polished frequently to maintain their shine.

2-Quart saucepan (with a matching lid): The big brother to the above-mentioned will make any newbie a kitchen heavyweight in no time. You'll earn your stripes in just a few attempts. Once again, having a lid will aid in those times when you're cooking rice and couscous.

4-Quart stock pot (with a matching lid): If pasta makes your heart go pitter-patter, then you'll definitely want to run out and buy this piece of cookware. A lid is especially useful with this pot since covering it will help bring your pasta water to a boil *much* faster. Thus, you can eat sooner.

Grill pan: If you don't have an outdoor grill, an alternative is a cast-iron grill pan. It's like a cast-iron pan, but it has ridges in it, like a grill.

8" × 8" Nonstick baking pan: We're all suckers for a little baking to make a kitchen smell like home sweet home.

9" × 13" Baking pan: This is a versatile, standard-sized pan that everyone should have. Use it to roast a chicken or vegetables, or to store meats in the fridge while marinating.

9" × 5" Loaf pan: Perfect for smaller servings . . . and loaves.

9" Pie dish: This dish comes in handy for baking the average pie, but it can also be used for roasting.

Nonstick baking sheet: For all of you bakingophiles, here is your chance to take your oven racks by storm. Whether you are in the mood for homemade cookies or a little savory dinner consisting of Margarita pizza you'll love having a baking sheet at your disposal.

Last but Not Least

Microwave-safe bowl: The bottom of most bowls will tell you if they are microwave-safe or not. Glass and ceramic, without any gold or silver adornment, are usually good options.

Measuring cups (liquid and dry): Measuring cups and measuring spoons are *de rigueur* for most recipes. We wouldn't want you "guesstimating" on the quantities, as we all remember that lecture from chemistry lab—never a good idea and we wouldn't want you to end up in the nurse's office. Liquid measuring cups are typically glass and pitcher-like and have red lines outlining the amounts of cups/ounces on the outside. Dry measuring cups are most often metal or plastic and come in separate "cups" with handles, most often labeled 1 cup, ½ cup, ¼ cup, and ⅓ cup.

Measuring spoons: Buy a set of spoons that range from ¼ teaspoon to 1 tablespoon. Use them to learn how much each measurement is just by sight. For example, if you need 1 teaspoon of cumin, first measure it into the spoon, then pour it into your palm and remember what it looks like. Soon, you won't need to scavenge through your drawers looking for the teaspoon!

Nested mixing bowls: This family of bowls, whether they are ceramic or metal, will aid you in the preparation of most of the recipes to follow. They will allow you the flexibility to combine ingredients from the most minuscule of spices to larger volumes of liquid. While you might be tempted to use your everyday cereal bowls, we'd highly recommend splurging on a set. Birthday, anyone? Anyone?

Colander: While it might look like a bike helmet for a cyclist with dreadlocks, it's actually a brilliant invention that prevents you from spilling half of your pasta into the sink while you carefully avoid burning yourself with scalding water. Consider it yet another fabulous accessory for your kitchen—and, much like shoes, they come in a rainbow of colors.

Cutting board: Wood cutting boards are great, but they can be a breeding ground for bacteria. Try thick plastic ones instead, and for sanitation purposes, have a separate cutting board for chicken, pork, fish, or anything that can cause contamination.

Plastic storage containers: There's a reason your mom loved those Tupperware parties. With your new cooking skills you're sure to have your own leftovers—not just the weekend meatloaf your mom is always pawning off. Secretly you know it stems from her inherent fear that you're surviving on pistachios and vodka.

Instant-read thermometer: Do not confuse this bad boy with the thermometer your mother kept in the "kids' bathroom." This distant cousin should *not* be inserted with the same flippancy as it was when you had your winter colds. To test the accuracy of your thermometer, simply bring a pot of water to a boil on your stove. When the water starts to bubble rapidly, insert the thermometer, making sure not to touch the sides of the pot, as you'll get an inaccurate read. If it reads 212°F, you're right on target. If it doesn't, most can be adjusted by turning the bolt that's just behind the face of the thermometer. (Or, if you're truly freaked out by any sort of gadget manipulation, try this trick: If your thermometer reads 202°F in boiling water, then you know it's 10 degrees off. So when a recipe calls for meat that reaches 180°F, you can feel safe eating it at 170°F, rather than risking roasting it until it becomes shoe leather.)

Staples: What You Really Need in Your Kitchen

Cooking is less daunting when one has a well-stocked kitchen. But it's important to understand what items keep and where they should be kept in order to prolong their shelf-life. General rule: If something has a putrid odor, has grown mold, or is discolored, your best bet is not using it. It's not high-school senior-year calculus (if you were brilliant enough to even consider taking this class, you're ahead of the pantry game . . .), but here are a variety of items to consider keeping on hand in a pantry, fridge, and freezer.

Pantry (AKA Dry Goods)

The average single girl living on her own for the first time (we don't count sorority houses or dorms) might not have a pantry (or one that she knows of . . .). If her living quarters are a minuscule studio apartment with no storage space for her overabundance of winter coats, much less food, there are a handful of ingenious pantry solutions. Baskets or bins above or below shelves is a perfect place to start. Many times there is space above the refrigerator that can be converted into additional storage space. Perhaps an old bookshelf that your parents handed down to you last summer could be placed in the kitchen as a makeshift pantry. Whatever the singleton pantry solution, it's always best to keep the following items on hand in order to simplify weekday cooking. The last thing any of us wants to do when we schlep home from work is go grocery shopping. By maintaining a well-stocked pantry, the clever Culinary Countess will save the most precious of commodities: her time.

- **Shallots:** Store in a cool, dry, unrefrigerated area. (A cute salad bowl you rarely use or a platter you inherited from your grandmother is a perfect home.)
- **Garlic:** Store in a cool, well-ventilated place, and do not refrigerate. Most garlic in supermarkets is sold in "heads," each of which is made up of twenty or so individual "cloves." Each "clove" must be peeled before use.
- **Onions:** Onions have a shorter shelf life than garlic and should not be stored for more than a few weeks in cool, dry, well-ventilated area. Do not refrigerate until cut. If they are sprouting, toss them.
- **Potatoes:** Store in a cool, dry place that doesn't get much light. You can keep potatoes, shallots, garlic, and onions in the same bowl. Most of our kitchens have at least one window (and thus, more light than our potatoes require); in this case, we recommend storing tubers and

similar items in a cupboard or pantry that shields them from direct sunlight.

• **Bread crumbs:** Seasoned bread crumbs have significantly more sodium. Stick to unseasoned ones and do the flavoring yourself.

- **Sesame seeds**
- **Cooking spray:** Extra-virgin olive oil only
- **Baking powder**
- **Baking soda**
- **Vanilla extract**
- **Cocoa powder**
- **Honey**
- **Splenda (for baking)**
- **Granulated sugar (white)**
- **Brown sugar**
- **Enriched flour**
- **Salt (kosher)**

• **Fresh ground black pepper:** Look for one of those disposable prefilled pepper grinders so you don't have to bother buying peppercorns and refilling a pepper mill. You'll find them right next to salt, pepper, and other spices in your grocery store.

• **Extra-virgin olive oil:** Oils can go rancid after a few months so buy a smaller bottle if you don't think you'll go through a large one. There are two types of olive oil you should keep on hand: one that is light in flavor (and color) for cooking (e.g., sautéing or roasting) and making salad dressing, and another higher quality one to leverage when you want the olive flavor to be robust. The label usually recommends what to use it for. This rich olive flavor is derived from a process called "first cold press," which means that these oils come from the first "squeeze" of the olives, thus are the most pure and authentic.

• **Sesame oil:** Used most often in Asian dishes, sesame oil is primarily a polyunsaturated fat, which makes this one a healthy oil.

• **Vinegars:** Rice wine, champagne, balsamic, and red wine.

- **Soy sauce**
- **Oyster sauce**
- **Rice:** Basmati, brown, white, or wild.

• **Pasta:** You've most likely already found that pasta is readily available in two varieties: fresh and dry. If you're planning on preparing pasta within a couple of days of purchase, fresh pastas are wonderful. Dry pastas, however, are ideal to have on hand for the evenings you can't decide what you're craving. Fusilli, rigatoni, penne, spaghetti, bow ties, angel hair, linguini, and orecchiette make a perfect base for various ingredients and sauces you may have in your refrigerator. Keep in mind that we're all about maximizing our health and nutrition. Therefore, if whole-wheat pasta is available in the variety of pasta we're craving, then whole-wheat it is.

• **Herbs and spices:** Dried herbs and spices lose their flavor after a few months so buy the smaller containers (a 2-ounce jar is perfect) to keep from wasting. A few that come in handy:

Basil	*Oregano*
Celery seed	*Paprika*
Cinnamon	*Rosemary*
Cumin	*Sage*
Curry	*Tarragon*
Dill	*Thyme*
Nutmeg	

Refrigerator

Many of the following items will be stored in your dry pantry and will be found unrefrigerated in your grocery store. Once they've been opened, however, they *must* be refrigerated. A few standard tricks of the trade in knowing when food has "gone bad": (1) it has mold growing on it, (2) its stench has permeated your refrigerator, (3) it looks a bit funky and you'd be hard pressed to get your dog to eat it. If you have to ask, it should go in the garbage. Food poisoning is not fun.

• **Salsa**

• **Salad dressing:** This includes homemade recipes from this book. Homemade vinaigrettes don't last as long (about 5 days) as bottled versions because they don't contain preservatives.

• **Teriyaki sauce**

• **Tomato paste:** Tomato paste is used as the base for homemade marina sauce and is available in small cans or sometimes a recloseable tube. They are typically found in the pasta sauce or canned tomato section of a grocery store.

• **Tomato sauce**

• **Roasted peppers**

• **Capers**

• **Mandarin oranges**

• **Chicken and/or vegetable broth:** We recommend the low-sodium 14.5-ounce cans, unless you're doubling a recipe. Broth freezes really well, too, so don't throw away 9 ounces if you only need 5.5.

• **Black olives**

• **Canned beans:** black, garbanzo, kidney, and cannellini

• **Canned tomatoes:** San Marzano tomatoes are delicious if you can find them. They come from Italy and have great flavor. Depending on what a recipe calls for, you can buy them diced, chopped, crushed, stewed, etc., etc., etc. For most recipes you can get by with crushed or diced, so keep those on hand. Also avoid cans that have added ingredients such as basil, pepper, or mushrooms, as these varieties contain higher levels of sodium. Also, though we're all about preaching the penny-pinching, if organic canned tomatoes are available, buy them.

- **Canned veggies:** Beets, corn, water chestnuts, hearts of palm, and artichoke hearts. Most other canned veggies are far less superior to fresh, whereas these few hold up well.
- **Polenta**
- **Green olives:** Jarred green olives in the condiment aisle are perfect. Avoid the olives "stuffed" with garlic, cheese, or pimentos (Spanish olives) as they contain not only unwanted flavors but also unneeded calories.
- **Large eggs:** A carton of fresh eggs (not cooked) will last 4 to 5 weeks past the sell-by date if they are stored properly in the refrigerator. It's always a good idea to use the egg tray, if one is available (they typically come with the refrigerator, or you can buy one). These egg containers separate the eggs and prevent them from breaking. That being the case, don't ever use broken or damaged eggs, as bacteria can easily spread through a cracked shell.
- **Fresh herbs:** Herbs can actually last over a week if stored properly. After washing them, wrap them loosely in a paper towel and store in a plastic bag. The paper towel pulls moisture away from the herbs, thus keeping them fresh longer.
- **Mustard:** Dijon, whole-grain, and yellow.
- **Hummus**
- **Mayonnaise**
- **Ketchup**
- **Barbecue sauce**
- **Butter (salted and unsalted)**
- **Minced ginger**
- **Minced garlic**
- **Hard cheeses:** A chunk of Parmesan or a block of aged Cheddar.
- **Jelly/jam**
- **Cream cheese**

Freezer

The swinging single girl never knows when the next late night at work is going to strike. The last thing she wants is to walk into her apartment and realize she has nothing to satiate her hunger except leftovers from last week's company picnic that she secretly boxed up when everyone was playing the last inning of the softball game. It will take only one evening of malnourishment to encourage her to keep the following items in her freezer to avoid another dietary disaster.

- **Corn**
- **Peas**
- **Ginger root:** Has almost an indefinite shelf-life when frozen.
- **Fruit**
- **Nuts:** Almonds, hazelnuts, pine nuts, pecans, and walnuts. Oils found in nuts, like any oil, can go rancid. Freezing nuts thwarts this process and improves their shelf life. Toasting nuts, after they've been frozen, will spruce up their freshness and flavor. Don't even bother thawing them; just toss 'em right into the oven. Buying nuts whole is always the best bet, as they can be chopped, minced, or diced according to each recipe. Almond slivers, however, are the exception to this rule, as we wouldn't encourage any girl to attempt slivering her almonds. That's about as productive as making your own sausage.
- **Meats:** Freezing meat offers you the freedom and flexibility to cook exactly what you're craving when you get home *without* making a pit stop at the grocery store before heading home. Just remember, when you freeze meats, use zip-top freezer bags to prevent frostbite, as meat that is stored improperly tends to lose its flavor and shelf life more rapidly. Try to use it within three to four months if it's raw when frozen, or one month if it's cooked.

- **Sausages**
- **Bacon/turkey bacon**
- **Beef:** Try to buy cuts with the words "loin" or "round" in them because they're the leanest and healthiest. Flank steak, sirloin, and extra-lean ground beef are great ways to go, too. Wrap cuts of meat in individual portions so you're not stuck trying to chisel one piece out of the bargain family pack.
- **Chicken:** Boneless, skinless breasts are the best option when it comes to your health. Wrap individual portions separately so you can easily grab just what you need from the freezer.
- **Pork:** Look for tenderloin, centerloin, Canadian bacon, or ham when you're in the mood for the other white meat.
- Shrimp
- Salted butter

In addition to meats and other frozen foods, you can also freeze your own meals from *The Little Black Apron*. Again, they're perfect for those evenings when you're not feeling up to task. Here are a few basic and ready-to-have-on-hand recipes that will add taste and decrease the amount of time spent preparing a meal, as you'll already have them in your freezer.

- **Sun-Dried Tomato Pesto, page 235:** Let the pesto thaw prior to using it.

- **Basil Pesto, page 231:** Let the pesto thaw prior to using it.

- **Mushroom Ragout, page 81:** Let thaw, then reheat in a skillet over medium low heat.

- **Caramelized Onions, page 84:** Let thaw, then reheat in a skillet over medium heat.

- **Almond-Olive Relish, page 230:** Let the relish thaw prior to using it.

- **Romesco Sauce, page 235:** Let the sauce thaw prior to using it.

- **Latin American Chimichurri Sauce, page 233:** Let the sauce thaw prior to using it.

- **Miso Marinade, page 233 (for Miso Marinated Halibut, page 133):** Let the marinade thaw prior to using it.

- **Basic Tomato Sauce, page 230:** Let thaw, then reheat in a sauce pot on medium heat, stirring often.

- **Pepperonata, page 234 (for Seared Pepperonata Tuna Steak, page 137):** Let thaw, then reheat in a skillet over medium heat, stirring often.

- **Pizza Dough, uncooked:** Follow cooking instructions on page 181.

- **Pizzas, cooked:** To freeze, wrap tightly in plastic wrap. Reheat, unwrapped, on a baking sheet in a 400°F oven until warm.

- **Frittatas (pages 140–45):** To freeze, wrap tightly in plastic wrap. Reheat, unwrapped, on a baking sheet in a 350°F oven for 15 minutes.

- **Chicken Enchiladas, page 118:** To freeze, wrap tightly with plastic wrap. To reheat, unwrap then cover with foil and bake on a 9" × 13" pan, in a 350°F oven for 30 minutes; uncover and bake 10 minutes more. You can also make just the sauce ahead of time and freeze for later use. Allow to thaw, then reheat in a saucepan over medium heat, stirring often.

- **Coconut Curry Chicken, page 116:** To freeze, wrap tightly with plastic wrap. To reheat, unwrap then cover with foil and bake in an 8" × 8" pan in a 350°F oven for 30 minutes. Or reheat over medium-low heat in a saucepan on the stove.

Julia Child

"I was 32 when I started cooking; up until then I just ate."

cooking for the single girl
meals for sunday through thursday nights

In chapters 4 through 8 we'll outline recipes for salads, veggies and sides, proteins, starches, and desserts in the hope that, with them, you will learn how to properly cook for yourself. Perhaps you'll even restore that beautiful Marin County mountain house or that tropical bungalow oasis you already have your eye on.

Since we work well with the shoe, jewelry, and handbag metaphors, we'll start painting the picture there. Think of *The Little Black Apron* like the little black dress, and each recipe as an accessory. We know it's not quite as glamorous, but you're well educated, so use your very expensive imagination.

The little black dress can be worn over and over again, sometimes twice in the same week to different functions with the same attendees. You are confident it will go unnoticed as a result of it being uniquely altered each time with accessories from your endless arsenal of jewelry, shoes, and handbags. Same concept with cooking. Each recipe can be accessorized in a spectrum of combinations in order to give your palate a wee bit of culinary variation.

Now, we don't count Fridays and Saturdays as "at-home-cooking" nights. Give us some credit; the sexy single girl should not cook on date nights. So throw on that little black dress and make some nice boy(s) pony up and take you out on the town—on one night, if not both. Paint it red for us.

But for those nights when it's just you, you shouldn't be relegated to Lucky Charms and Diet Coke. The four basic food groups unfortunately do not consist of wine, cheese, chocolate, and coffee. The three of us would be more than willing to live a life of gluttonous pleasure on the aforementioned, but we were hard pressed to locate a food-guide pyramid outlining the nutritional benefits of leading a life based on sin consumption. And while we can all point fingers at a complacent government, we have to give credit where credit is due. The food-guide pyramid that the USDA updated in 2005 is very different from the one we learned back in elementary school. (Take a look at the Web site *www.mypyramid.gov* for more information.)

The food-guide pyramid illustrates the food groups we need to consume each day, and in what quantities, to maintain optimal health. The width of the various bands indicates how much you should eat every day: Foods with thicker bands should be consumed in higher quantities. Fats are a very thin band, which means you should consume small amounts. The number of servings you need from each food group depends on the number of calories your body needs, which is based on a number of factors such as age, gender, height, weight, activity level, and metabolism. (Don't rack your lovely little brain to learn even more facts and figures. Mypyramid.gov outlines how many servings you need from each group.)

Keep in mind that eating a healthy diet doesn't just mean eating nutritious foods. Variety is an essential part of a balanced diet. Think about it. Eating carrots every day does not guarantee that your diet is healthy. Different foods provide different nutrients—for example, orange vegetables are high in beta carotene, whereas dark green vegetables are high in iron and vitamin E. Someone who eats only carrots would be missing out on these vitamins and minerals.

So, how do you know if you're eating a healthy diet? You should be eating foods from every food group—grains, vegetables, fruits, milk, meat, and beans—each day. Understanding your eating habits, as well as the nutritional value of the food groups in the pyramid, is critical for the savvy bachelorette. Nutrition is at the core of a wholesome and balanced life.

Depending on your definition of "wholesome," the recipes that follow provide you with the foundation to take your nutrition into your own hands. Each recipe includes the nutritional contents of its ingredients: folate, fiber, antioxidants, calcium, and omega-3s; because we're all not getting any younger, we also note whether a recipe is low-fat (less than 3 grams per serving) and whether it's a good source of whole grains. In addition, each chapter focuses on a specific set of dietary needs and outlines the benefits of those particular nutrients along with some other nutritional pitfalls to avoid. By understanding the nutritional benefits of each recipe, our hope is that the once uneducated and ambivalent nutrition-newbie will transform into a well-versed and educated cook.

RECIPE NUTRITION

Recipes marked with the following labels contain at least one food that is a healthy supplier of that nutrient.

ANTIOXIDANTS
CALCIUM
FIBER
FOLATE
LOW-FAT
OMEGA-3
WHOLE GRAINS

Fran Lebowitz

"Food is an important part of a balanced diet."

salads
green like envy or emeralds

Emeralds and salads. What can we say except that we love them? Well, we love all jewelry and most food, but these precious natural wonders are particularly dear to our hearts. Perhaps it's their color, royal and proud, illuminating *green*.

If there is one way we can convince you that this most precious of gems is green for a reason, we'll turn to salads. The way to parlay the correlation between these two is through the following maxims. We'll keep it simple.

1. The more the merrier.
2. The bigger the better.
3. The greener the more precious.
4. Uncut or uncooked, it doesn't matter.
5. You can never go wrong having more.
6. Satiates most of your desires.
7. They're good to wear/eat in all seasons.
8. Learn to love them all. (Shapes, cuts, styles, and varieties.)
9. Your friends will be jealous of your uncanny understanding of them.
10. They provide unparalleled nutritional benefits to your health as they contain both folate and fiber. (Okay, well, emeralds provide a mental health benefit. . . .)

Folate: As Luck Would Have It

Remember sitting at the table until you finished your vegetables, despite requesting that your mother refrain from preparing anything greener than iceberg lettuce with Ranch dressing? It seems that once again, our mothers were right. Consider this maternal instinct an understanding of "survival of the fittest." Our mothers understood that lurking within the nutritional genetic makeup of these most repulsive of greens was folate, which is critical to our health.

Folate is found naturally in fruits and vegetables such as spinach, broccoli, kiwis, and asparagus. Enough folate in your diet may reduce the risk of having a child with a brain or spinal cord birth defect (although this is far from the only reason we need folate—it is integrally involved in DNA and making new cells). No need to panic and take four pregnancy tests in a row, paranoid as you may be. As much as we might hate to admit that we aren't in control of all aspects of our lives, many pregnancies are not planned. (Shocker.) And even if they are, many women do not realize they're pregnant until it's a month or two into the pregnancy. In order to prevent potential birth defects, women need adequate folate/folic acid— 400 micrograms (mcg) per day.

Thanks to the wonders of technology, many foods—namely cereals, rice, pasta, and breads—are now folate-enriched. In 1998, the United States government mandated that all enriched grain and grain products produced in the United States be fortified with folic acid, the supplement form of folate, to help ensure that all women receive an adequate amount of the nutrient. Whether or not you consider this mandate a Darwinist micromanaging conspiracy on the part of the U.S. government is your call. While folic acid is actually better absorbed than the natural folate found in vegetables, you should not harbor your vegetable conspiracy theory. It's still a good idea to get folate directly from the food source to maintain a healthy diet, since greens provide many other nutritional benefits (such as fiber, vitamins, and minerals). The recipes in this chapter include myriad ingredients that are amazing sources of folate.

Just in case you weren't confused enough, too much folate in your diet can mask a vitamin B_{12} deficiency. But don't panic and start building a concrete shelter in the backyard as a result of the "Green Scare" to avoid your veggies. Remember, a *balanced* diet is always the key (B_{12} deficiency is often of most concern in vegetarians and vegans). We know, we know, we just told you to consume folate. We're as bad as French grammar rules.

These are the rules for conjugating the verb *manger* (to eat). Please note, however, there are 117 slight odd loopholes that we like to call "exceptions" to conjugating *manger*. And you wonder why it took you eight consecutive years

Healthy Suppliers of Folate/Folic Acid

Food	Micrograms (mcg) per serving
1 cup Kellogg's Smart Start cereal	402
1⅓ cups Total cereal	400
½ cup cooked enriched medium-grain white rice	225
½ cup cooked lentils	180
1 cup boiled collard greens	177
1 cup canned chickpeas	161
2 ounces uncooked enriched spaghetti	135
½ cup cooked spinach	132
1 medium papaya	116
1 cup cooked frozen peas	94
4 spears asparagus	88
½ cup avocado	71
½ cup beets	68
1 cup romaine lettuce	64
½ cup broccoli	57
1 cup kiwi	44

of French language class just to sputter out three sentences in a row.

Speaking of the French, another recent study showed that women who consume more than two alcoholic beverages per week (AKA a glass

Food Combos to Ensure Your 100% Daily Folate

One apple + 1 cup Brussels sprouts + 1 cup spinach + ½ cup barley

1 cup Kellogg's Smart Start or 1 cup Product 19 or 1⅓ cups Total cereals

¾ cup cooked lentils in soup with ½ cup cooked spinach

1 cup cooked pasta + ¼ cup sunflower seeds + 1 cup frozen peas

2 tablespoons peanut butter + 1 English muffin + 1 papaya + 1 cup Honey Nut Cheerios

4 asparagus spears + 2 cups romaine lettuce + ½ cup cooked white rice

of wine after a long, hard, demoralizing day at the office) and have a diet low in folate have an increased risk of ovarian cancer. If the thought of giving up that smooth, wonderful Cabernet is not enough to make you start to broaden your green horizon, perhaps the fact that a diet low in folate is also associated with an increased risk of heart disease will. We knew we'd get you, somehow, but giving up wine? *Never.*

Fiber's Tell-All Tale

There are occasions in life when we're embarrassed for one reason or another. Going bra shopping for the first time, for instance. That particular day was almost as painful as your bikini wax last weekend in the utility closet of the shady nail joint that recently opened down the street. (How could any girl pass up $19.99 for both a bikini and lip wax?) However, on *that* torturous day well over a decade ago, your mother called every living female relative to share the good news—you had finally grown breasts. That Saturday afternoon was her day to show you (and the mosquito bites) off to the world. Blushing pubescent girls everywhere were shuttled to the nearest department store—two hours of humiliation that lasted for nearly all of your teenage years—to go bra shopping. Most mothers insist on coming in and out of the dressing room for what seemed to be a duration of time longer than your first pediatrician visit with pubic hair.

It wasn't until you realized that more embarrassing events would transpire over the course of high school, certainly college, and your first job, that you realized your first day in the Bloomingdale's undergarments section was the least of your problems.

One such mortifying episode happens to you almost every morning between 9:30 and 10:30 in the ladies' restroom after your morning cup of Joe kicks in. You know what we're talking about.

Sure, you'll never admit that you "go" anywhere besides the privacy and comfort of your own home, but let's be honest: Shit happens. You try to time it perfectly, but somehow, without fail, your five minutes of bathroom solitude is always interrupted. Someone walks into the stall next to yours and breaks your concentration.

Finally she leaves the restroom. Once again, you are able to attend to your business, and you feel as if you've lost five pounds. It's a good day. Immediately, you wonder how to make this miracle weight loss a daily occurrence. The answer is *fiber*.

Fiber, both insoluble and soluble, is important for a variety of reasons, but we'll begin with the most obvious: It keeps you regular. You always knew there was a correlation between eating a salad for dinner and feeling skinnier the next day. Integrating fruits, vegetables, whole grains, and legumes into your diet will inevitably result in healthier "morning inspirations." Insoluble fiber, the fiber found in wheat, bran, and many types of vegetables, increases the bulking process in your body, aiding in the movement of food through your digestive system. High-fiber diets also can help prevent diverticulitis, or the formation of small pouches in your intes-tines, by maintaining the functioning of the gastrointestinal tract.

In addition to maintaining regularity and preventing constipation, fiber aids in filling you up, making it essential for weight loss and weight maintenance. If that's not enough to get your attention, a diet high in soluble fiber, such as that found in oats, beans, and some fruit, also helps decrease the risk of heart disease. Soluble fiber acts like a scouring agent, but in your circulatory system. These soluble fibers clear out harmful LDL ("bad") cholesterol before it adheres to the walls of your arteries.

Daily Fiber Recommendations

The USDA recommends 25 grams of fiber for women under age fifty every day. Rather than counting grams, however, aim for these Fiber Daily Aspirations:

Choose at least half of your grains from the whole grains.

Eat two to three servings of fruit per day. (The skin of fruit often contains a lot of fiber. However, any whole fruit will provide a healthy supply of fiber, which is usually lost when it's made into juice.)

Eat four to six servings of vegetables per day.

Eat at least three servings of beans per week.

In Case You Need Some Ideas . . .

- Eat more whole grains

  Whole-wheat bread   *Whole-wheat crackers*

  Oatmeal   *Couscous (whole-wheat)*

  Brown rice   *Whole-wheat pasta*

  Whole-grain cereal   *Barley*

- Eat more fruit

  Apples   *Melon*

  Bananas   *Oranges*

  Cherries   *Pears*

  Grapes   *Raisins*

  Kiwi

- Eat more vegetables

  Leafy greens   *Spinach*

  Tomato   *Carrots*

  Mushrooms   *Asparagus*

  Broccoli   *Zucchini*

  Cauliflower   *Corn*

- Eat more legumes

  Black beans   *Lentils*

  Garbanzo beans   *Pinto beans*

  Kidney beans   *Split peas*

Much can be said about humiliation during puberty or even being caught in your morning inspirational act, but we're confident that there is nothing embarrassing about preventing various types of cancer, diabetes, and heart disease—all benefits of a diet high in fiber. Therefore, be bold the next time your cubicle mate steps into the neighboring stall. Wish her well, hoping that she's consumed her daily dose of fiber.

Note: All dressing recipes should make at least several days' worth of dressing. Remember the portion size discussion in Chapter 1—a serving of salad dressing should be about 1 tablespoon, or half a Ping-Pong ball.

Easiest Ever Mixed Green Salad with Lemon Vinaigrette

1. Combine the first four ingredients and toss well.

2. Using a vegetable peeler, shave about 5 pieces of cheese off of a wedge.

3. Top the salad with shaved cheese.

QUICKIE

● *Mesclun is a mix of baby lettuces. The mixture varies depending on your store but often includes arugula, mizuna, frizee, an radicchio.*

NUTRIENTS
Antioxidants
Calcium
Folate

3 cups mesclun mix (mixed baby greens, usually sold in bulk in most grocery stores)

1 teaspoon fresh lemon juice (from about half a lemon))

½ tablespoon good extra-virgin olive oil

Salt and pepper to taste

Shaved Parmesan cheese

COOKING ACCESSORIES
Bowl
Vegetable peeler

Iceberg Wedge with Blue Cheese Vinaigrette

NUTRIENTS
Antioxidants
Calcium
Fiber
Folate

VINAIGRETTE:

1 ounce crumbled blue cheese

1 tablespoon champagne vinegar

2 tablespoons extra-virgin olive oil

½ tablespoon chopped fresh Italian (flat-leaf) parsley

⅛ teaspoon salt

⅛ teaspoon ground black pepper

COOKING ACCESSORIES

Blender or food processor

Chef's knife

7" Sauté pan or nonstick baking sheet

Bowl

1. Combine the first three ingredients in a blender or food processor and process until smooth, about 5 to 7 seconds.

2. Stir in the parsley, salt, and pepper.

SALON:

SALAD:

¼ head of iceberg lettuce, sliced lengthwise from the head

¼ small apple (or nectarine during summer), sliced into wedges

¼ cup toasted walnuts (a handful)

1. Remove any discolored or wilted leaves from the lettuce. Make sure the lettuce is dry; otherwise the dressing will run right off.

2. In a separate bowl, toss the apple wedges and walnuts with about a teaspoon of the vinaigrette.

3. Drizzle about 2 tablespoons of the vinaigrette over the wedge of iceberg. Top with the apples and walnuts.

QUICKIES

- *The vinaigrette can be made ahead of time. It will keep, covered, in the fridge for 3 to 4 days.*

- *Toast nuts on a baking sheet in a 300°F oven for a few minutes. They are done cooking as soon as you can smell them. Overcooking them will burn their oils and they'll become bitter. You can also toast them in a dry sauté pan (without oil) on the stove; toss them occasionally.*

- *There will be extra lettuce, so use the leftovers for another salad tomorrow, or throw some on a turkey sandwich and take it to work for a healthy lunch. Try a lettuce wrap: Fill up a piece of lettuce with sliced chicken breast and drizzle with leftover blue cheese vinaigrette!*

Tomato, Avocado, and Corn Salad with Citrus Vinaigrette

1. Coat a 7" sauté pan or other small skillet with a thin layer of olive oil and heat it over medium high heat.

2. Sauté the corn about 5 minutes, remove from heat, and let it cool.

3. In a bowl, toss the tomatoes, avocado, corn with juices, olive oil, salt, and pepper.

4. Top with basil.

QUICKIES

● *Peeling and seeding an avocado is easy! Insert a knife at the top of the avocado and cut down until it reaches the seed, then run the knife around the entire avocado. Twist the two halves in opposite directions until they separate. To remove the seed, carefully hit the seed with the blade of the knife, so that the blade sticks in the seed. Then, holding the half in your other hand, twist it until the seed pops out. Carefully pull the seed off the knife with a dish towel. Now you're left with two seedless halves. To peel them, run a spoon right between the skin and the flesh of the avocado.*

● *Keep your cut avocados green by squeezing a little lemon juice on them before wrapping in plastic wrap or putting in an airtight container.*

NUTRIENTS
Antioxidants
Fiber
Folate
Whole Grain

Extra virgin olive oil for sautéing

¼ cup frozen corn

1 ripe tomato, cut into bite-size chunks

¼ avocado, cut into bite-size chunks

1 teaspoon lemon juice

1 teaspoon orange juice

1 teaspoon lime juice

2 tablespoons extra-virgin olive oil

Salt and pepper to taste

½ tablespoon fresh basil, leaves torn from stems and roughly chopped

COOKING ACCESSORIES
Chef's knife
7" Sauté pan
Bowl

Arugula with Pears, Gorgonzola, and Champagne Vinaigrette

NUTRIENTS
Antioxidants
Calcium
Fiber
Folate

2 cups arugula

¼ pear, cut into bite-size chunks

¼ tablespoon champagne vinegar

1 tablespoon extra-virgin olive oil

Salt and pepper to taste

1 tablespoon crumbled Gorgonzola

1. Toss the arugula and pears in a bowl with the vinegar, oil, salt, and pepper.

2. Top with the crumbled Gorgonzola.

QUICKIES

- *Arugula, also called rocket, is a type of lettuce with a delicious peppery flavor. Look for it in your grocery store with other lettuces, often near the spinach.*

- *As with avocados, keep your cut pears from browning by squeezing a little lemon juice on them. The acid stops oxidation and prevents browning.*

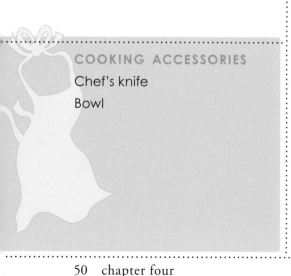

COOKING ACCESSORIES

Chef's knife

Bowl

Avocado and Fennel Salad with Grapefruit Vinaigrette

1. Cut the quarter fennel bulb in half to remove the core. Discard the core, then slice the bulb as thinly as possible.

2. Cut the grapefruit in half. Cut one half into supremes; reserve the other half for juice for the vinaigrette.

3. Arrange the watercress on a plate; top with the avocado, fennel, and grapefruit supremes. Sprinkle with salt and pepper.

4. Squeeze 1 tablespoon of juice from the remaining grapefruit. Drizzle the juice and the olive oil on top of the salad.

QUICKIES

- *Supremes: Using a knife, cut off the top and bottom of the grapefruit, then peel from top to bottom using the knife so that no pith (the white part between the fruit and the skin) remains on the fruit. Cut right along the membranes, between each section of fruit, so that each section of the grapefruit comes out.*

- *Fennel is a bulb that is found in the produce section, usually near other root veggies and cabbages. It has long green stalks and a white base. At the top of the stalks are the " fronds," which can be used as a garnish. It has a slight licorice flavor and can be used raw or cooked.*

- *To peel an avocado and to keep it from browning, see page 49.*

NUTRIENTS
Antioxidants
Calcium
Fiber
Folate

¼ fennel bulb
1 grapefruit
1 cup watercress
½ avocado, sliced
Salt and pepper
½ tablespoon extra-virgin olive oil

COOKING ACCESSORIES
Chef's knife

Classic Caprese

NUTRIENTS
Antioxidants
Calcium

1 ripe tomato, cut into ½" slices
4 slices fresh mozzarella
Salt and pepper
5 fresh basil leaves, stems removed
½ tablespoon extra-virgin olive oil

1. Arrange the tomato slices and mozzarella slices, alternating, on a plate. Sprinkle with salt and pepper.

2. Arrange the basil leaves on top.

3. Drizzle with the olive oil.

QUICKIE

- *Mozzarella balls work well too. They are called bocconcini and are bite-sized.*

COOKING ACCESSORIES
Chef's knife

Cole Slaw

1. Whisk together the crème fraiche, mayonnaise, vinegar, mustard, celery seed, and oregano in a bowl.

2. Add the cabbage, scallions, salt, and pepper. Combine well and let sit, refrigerated, for at least 20 minutes before serving.

QUICKIES

- *For a lower-fat alternative to crème fraiche or sour cream, replace with low-fat or nonfat sour cream.*

- *If you buy a whole cabbage, peel off the outer leaves, then slice through the root into quarters lengthwise. Cut out the root on an angle. Using a very sharp chef's knife, cut into shreds, or shred it in a food processor.*

NUTRIENTS
Antioxidants
Calcium
Fiber
Folate

1 tablespoon crème fraiche or sour cream

1 tablespoon low-fat mayonnaise

½ tablespoon red wine vinegar

½ teaspoon whole-grain mustard

¼ teaspoon celery seed

⅛ teaspoon dried oregano

1 cup pre-shredded cabbage

¼ scallion or green onion, thinly sliced. Use both the green and white parts, but remember to trim off the root.

Salt and pepper

COOKING ACCESSORIES
Whisk
Chef's knife
Bowl

Heirloom Tomato, Bocconcini, and Olive Tapenade

1 or 2 heirloom tomatoes, depending on their size, sliced into ¼" to ½" rounds. You'll want to end up with about four rounds, or a small handful's worth.

2 bocconcini (mozzarella balls), cut in half

2 teaspoons olive tapenade (store-bought versions are great)

½ teaspoon balsamic vinegar

Fresh ground black pepper to taste

COOKING ACCESSORIES
Chef's knife

1. Arrange the tomatoes and bocconcini on a plate.

2. Dollop the tapenade on top.

3. Drizzle with the balsamic vinegar and sprinkle with pepper.

QUICKIES

- *Late summer is when tomatoes are at their peak, especially heirlooms.*

- *Heirloom tomatoes (or other heirloom vegetable varieties) come from seeds that are about fifty years old. They are much more full-flavored and, heirloom tomatoes especially, come in beautiful colors and shapes.*

- *Tapenade is a purée of olives, sometimes including herbs and other flavorings like capers. You can find it in the condiment aisle near other olives.*

Grilled Radicchio and Arugula Salad with Lemon Vinaigrette

1. Heat a grill or a grill pan on medium high heat.

2. Combine 1 teaspoon of the olive oil with the smashed garlic clove in a small dish and stir, thus creating garlic oil.

3. Brush the radicchio quarters with the garlic oil and season with salt and pepper.

4. Grill the radicchio on each side until there are grill marks and each piece is wilted but not mushy.

5. Remove the radicchio from the grill and toss with the arugula, lemon juice, and remaining 1 tablespoon olive oil.

6. Top with the olives.

QUICKIE

- *To get rid of the scent of garlic from your hands, slice a lemon in half and rub it all over. The acid in the juice helps remove the odor.*

NUTRIENTS
Antioxidants
Calcium
Folate

1 teaspoon extra-virgin olive oil

1 clove garlic, smashed with the side of a knife

½ head radicchio, any outer wilted leaves removed, cut into quarters lengthwise

Salt and pepper

1 cup arugula

½ tablespoon lemon juice

1 tablespoon extra-virgin olive oil

1 tablespoon niçoise olives (or your favorite variety), chopped

COOKING ACCESSORIES
Chef's knife
Small dish
Brush
Grill pan
Bowl

Vegetable Slaw with Sesame Vinaigrette

NUTRIENTS
Antioxidants
Fiber
Folate
Low-fat

⅓ cup pre-shredded cabbage

⅓ cup pre-shredded carrots

⅓ cup julienned red bell pepper

⅓ cup julienned cucumber

1 tablespoon rice wine vinegar

½ tablespoons sugar or sugar substi-
    tute (such as Splenda)

¼ teaspoon sesame oil

2 teaspoons chopped fresh cilantro

Salt and pepper to taste

COOKING ACCESSORIES
Chef's knife
Bowl

Combine all ingredients and toss well.

QUICKIES

- *To julienne a red bell pepper, first cut off the top and bottom. Then make one cut from top to bottom, and then run the knife along the inside to remove the core of the pepper and seeds. Now cut the pepper into thin strips, about ¼" thick.*

- *To julienne a cucumber, first cut a 2–3 inch section from the cuc and stand it up. Slice it into ¼" "planks." Then rotate it and cut in the other direction, making the cuts perpendicular to the first set, so you end up with pieces that resemble matchsticks.*

Spinach and Roasted Peppers *with Balsamic-Herb Vinaigrette*

In a small bowl, whisk all vinaigrette ingredients together vigorously until well combined, about 10 seconds.

SALAD:

3 cups spinach leaves (most grocery stores sell spinach in bulk so you can buy the amount you want)

1 roasted red pepper, cut into thin strips. You'll want about ¼ cup.

In a large bowl toss the spinach and roasted peppers with about ¾ tablespoon of the vinaigrette. Save the leftover vinaigrette for another salad or drizzle it over chicken.

QUICKIES

- *We recommend buying roasted red peppers in a jar rather than taking the time to roast your own.*
- *To chop herbs, gather them up into a bundle together and chop with a chef's knife.*
- *Italian flat-leaf parsley has much better flavor than curly parsley. It's usually next to curly parsley in the grocery store, and, yes, it has flat leaves, which are pretty easy to distinguish.*
- *To get rid of the scent of garlic from your hands, slice a lemon in half and rub it all over. The acid in the juice helps remove the odor.*

NUTRIENTS
Antioxidants
Calcium
Fiber
Folate

VINAIGRETTE:

1 tablespoon balsamic vinegar

1 small clove garlic, chopped (or use a garlic press), about ¼ teaspoon

1 teaspoon Dijon mustard

1 teaspoon chopped fresh rosemary

1 teaspoon finely chopped thyme

2 teaspoons finely chopped fresh Italian flat-leaf parsley

2 to 3 tablespoons extra-virgin olive oil

⅛ teaspoon salt

Pinch of fresh ground black pepper

COOKING ACCESSORIES
Garlic press (optional)
Whisk
Small bowl
Chef's knife
Large bowl

Chopped Vegetable Salad with Lemon Vinaigrette

VINAIGRETTE:

2 teaspoons fresh lemon juice

2 teaspoons extra-virgin olive oil

Salt and pepper to taste

COOKING ACCESSORIES

Small bowl

Whisk

Chef's knife

Large bowl

In a small bowl whisk all vinaigrette ingredients together vigorously until well combined, about 10 seconds.

SALAD:

¼ small English cucumber, cut into ¼" rounds. You'll want 4 to 5 rounds.

½ small tomato, cut into wedges

½ small yellow bell pepper, cut into ½"-wide strips

1 tablespoon red onion, roughly chopped

1 handful kalamata olives, pitted

1 tablespoon crumbled feta cheese

2 teaspoons oregano, chopped

In a large bowl combine all ingredients and toss with the vinaigrette.

QUICKIES

- *Buy European or English cucumbers. They're the ones that are wrapped in plastic, right next to the American versions that have a waxy coating on the skin. The skin is thin so there is no need to peel it and there are no seeds so you don't need to scoop them out.*

- *Originating in Greece, feta cheese is classically made from sheep or goat milk, but today is often made from cow milk as well. (The sheep and goat milk varieties have a superior flavor, however, so look for those.) The cheese is stored in a salty brine and has a tangy flavor. Two brands to try are Mt. Vikos or Valbreso.*

Taco Salad with Cilantro Vinaigrette

1. Cut off and discard the bottom inch of the cilantro stems. Rinse the cilantro and pat dry with a paper towel.

2. Blend the cilantro and all remaining vinaigrette ingredients in a blender or food processor until smooth.

SALAD:

½ heart of romaine

½ small tomato, cut into wedges

¼ ripe avocado, cut into ½" chunks

½ small scallion or green onion, thinly sliced. Use both the green and white parts, but remember to trim off the root.

2 tablespoons canned black beans, drained

5 tortilla chips (restaurant-style chips, like Casa Sanchez)

Small handful, about 2 tablespoons, shredded Monterey jack cheese

Slice the romaine in half lengthwise, then crosswise into ½" strips. Toss the romaine, tomato, avocado, scallion, and beans with 1 to 2 tablespoons of the vinaigrette. Top the salad with tortilla chips and cheese.

QUICKIES

- *If you don't think you'll eat the entire salad, dress only the portion you'll have. Keep the remaining salad in the fridge and dress it when you're ready to eat it.*

- *Cilantro looks similar to Italian parsley, and as luck would have it they're usually next to each other in the supermarket. Cilantro has relatively tender and flavorful stems, so, except for the bottom inch or so, it's okay to use the stems in a food processor.*

- *Ancho chilies, deep red in color with a rich flavor, are dried versions of poblano chilies. Ancho chili powder is simply finely ground ancho chilies.*

NUTRIENTS
Antioxidants
Calcium
Fiber
Folate

VINAIGRETTE:

¼ bunch fresh cilantro

½ tablespoon red wine vinegar

½ tablespoon lime juice, from about half a lime

½ clove garlic, chopped (or use a garlic press), about ¼ teaspoon

½ tablespoon chopped red onion

¼ teaspoon ground cumin

⅛ teaspoon ground ancho chili powder (can be found in the spice aisle of most supermarkets)

2 tablespoons light extra-virgin olive oil

Salt and pepper to taste

COOKING ACCESSORIES
Garlic press (optional)
Chef's knife
Blender or food processor
Bowl

Sweet and Sour Cucumber Salad

NUTRIENTS
Antioxidants
Low-fat

¼ to ½ English cucumber, sliced into ¼" rounds

1 small handful very thinly sliced red onion

1 teaspoon chopped fresh mint

½ tablespoon sugar (Splenda can be substituted)

1 tablespoon unseasoned rice wine vinegar

Salt to taste

COOKING ACCESSORIES
Chef's knife
Bowl

Combine all ingredients well in a bowl.

QUICKIES

- *For an Asian-inspired version, add 1 teaspoon minced fresh ginger, ½ tablespoon chopped fresh basil, and ½ teaspoon chili garlic sauce.*

- *Buy European or English cucumbers. They're the ones that are wrapped in plastic, right next to the American versions that have a waxy coating on the skin. The skin is thin so there is no need to peel it and there are no seeds so you don't need to scoop them out.*

Fennel and Apple Salad

1. Trim off the root end and any green stalks on the fennel bulb and discard them. Slice the bulb from top to bottom into very thin slices.

2. Combine the first seven ingredients well in a bowl.

3. Mound the salad over a bed of the arugula.

QUICKIES

- *Fennel is a bulb that is found in the produce section, usually near other root veggies and cabbages. It has long green stalks and a white base. At the top of the stalks are the "fronds," which can be used as a garnish. It has a slight licorice flavor and can be used raw or cooked.*

- *Arugula, also called rocket, is a type of lettuce with a delicious peppery flavor. Look for it in your grocery store with other lettuces, often near the spinach.*

NUTRIENTS
Antioxidants
Calcium
Fiber
Folate
Low-fat

½ small fennel bulb

½ small Granny Smith apple (or whatever your favorite variety is), chopped into bite-sized pieces

1 teaspoon chopped fresh chives

1 tablespoon sugar (Splenda can be substituted)

1 tablespoon cider vinegar

Pinch of salt

Pinch of freshly ground black pepper

1 cup arugula

COOKING ACCESSORIES
Chef's knife
Bowl

Waldorf Salad

NUTRIENTS
Antioxidants
Calcium*
Fiber
Folate
Omega-3

*contains calcium only if made with yogurt

½ Granny Smith apple (or whatever your favorite variety is)

½ rib of celery

1 tablespoon walnuts (small handful), toasted

1 teaspoon pitted dates, roughly chopped (raisins can be substituted)

2 tablespoons plain yogurt or mayonnaise

½ tablespoon lemon juice (from one-quarter to one-half of a lemon)

1 teaspoon chopped fresh tarragon

Salt and pepper to taste

COOKING ACCESSORIES

7" Sauté pan or nonstick baking sheet

Chef's knife

Bowl

1. Cut the apple into wedges and remove and discard the core. Then cut the apple crosswise into ¼" pieces.

2. Slice the celery crosswise into ¼" pieces.

3. Combine the apple, celery, and remaining ingredients in a bowl and mix well.

QUICKIES

- *For fewer calories, switch out the mayo or yogurt for low- or non-fat mayonnaise or yogurt.*

- *Toast nuts on a baking sheet in a 300°F oven for just a few minutes. They are done cooking as soon as you can smell them. Overcooking them will burn their oils and they'll become bitter. You can also toast them in a dry pan (without oil) on the stove; toss them occasionally.*

- *Cutting something "crosswise" means to cut it against its natural top-to-bottom direction. For example, when cutting a carrot crosswise, you'll end up with coin-shaped pieces.*

Winter Fruit Salad with Toasted Cashews

In a bowl, combine all ingredients and mix well.

QUICKIES

- *If you make extra fruit salad, refrigerate it and save it for breakfast over yogurt!*

- *Toast nuts on a baking sheet in a 300°F oven for just a few minutes. They are done cooking as soon as you can smell them. Overcooking them will burn their oils and they'll become bitter. You can also toast them in a dry pan (without oil) on the stove; toss them occasionally.*

- *Cutting something "crosswise" means to cut it against its natural top-to-bottom direction. For example, when cutting a carrot crosswise, you'll end up with coin-shaped pieces.*

NUTRIENTS

Antioxidants
Fiber
Folate

½ kiwi, peeled, cut into ¼" rounds

¼ Fuji apple, cut into ¼" wedges and cored

¼ banana, cut crosswise into ¼" rounds

¼ pear, cut into ¼" wedges and cored

½ teaspoon fresh lemon juice

1 tablespoon toasted cashews, about a small handful

COOKING ACCESSORIES

Chef's knife

7" Sauté pan or nonstick baking sheet

Bowl

Summer Fruit Salad with Mint

NUTRIENTS
Antioxidants
Fiber
Folate
Low-fat

¼ nectarine, cut into ¼" wedges

2 large strawberries, stemmed and quartered

¼ banana, cut crosswise into ¼" rounds

¼ mango, cut into ¼" strips

Juice of ¼ lime

½ teaspoon fresh mint, chopped

COOKING ACCESSORIES
Chef's knife
Bowl

In a bowl combine all ingredients and mix well.

QUICKIES

- *To remove the pit from a nectarine, start at the stem end and run a knife around the whole fruit, cutting all the way down to the pit. Gently twist the two halves apart and the pit can be popped out. If it doesn't easily come out, carefully cut around it with the tip of a paring knife.*

- *To peel a mango, cut off the very top and the very bottom so that it stands flat on your cutting board. Starting at the top, peel it by running your knife down to the bottom, just in between the skin and the flesh of the fruit so that you peel the skin off in strips Repeat around the whole fruit until all of the skin is removed. The seed is flat and runs through the middle, so cut along each side of it to get the fruit off.*

- *Cutting something "crosswise" means to cut it against its natural top-to-bottom direction. For example, when cutting a carrot crosswise, you'll end up with coin-shaped pieces.*

Baby Greens *with Artichokes, Hazelnuts, Parmesan, and Lemon*

1. In a bowl, toss the greens and artichoke hearts with the lemon juice and olive oil and season with salt and pepper.

2. Top with the nuts and cheese.

QUICKIES

- *Hazelnuts are also called filberts.*
- *Check the salad bar at your grocery store for artichokes since you need only a small amount.*
- *Toast nuts on a baking sheet in a 300°F oven for just a few minutes. They are done cooking as soon as you can smell them. Overcooking them will burn their oils and they'll become bitter. You can also toast them in a dry pan (without oil) on the stove; toss them occasionally.*

NUTRIENTS

Antioxidants
Calcium
Fiber
Folate
Omega-3

2 cups baby greens

¼ cup quartered artichoke hearts (canned in water, not oil), about 1½ hearts

Juice of half a lemon

½ tablespoon good extra-virgin olive oil

Salt and pepper to taste

2 teaspoons toasted hazelnuts, coarsely chopped

1 tablespoon grated Parmesan (or shaved from a block using a vegetable peeler)

COOKING ACCESSORIES

Chef's knife

7" Sauté pan or nonstick baking sheet

Grater or vegetable peeler

Bowl

Doug Larson

"Life expectancy would grow by leaps and bounds if green vegetables smelled as good as bacon."

CHAPTER FIVE

veggies and sides
it's what's inside that counts

We've all been reminded at some point in our lives that "It's what's inside that counts." Those of us who wore glasses, were ridden with horrific acne, and spent many humiliating hours rocking out with our headgear—well, we weren't believers.

No matter how many times our best friends and mothers tried convincing us that it was our inner beauty that counted, we balked at their audacity. With time, however, the acne cleared, the glasses were lost and replaced with contacts, and the teeth transformed from looking like a fifty-six-year-old British man's to resembling a perfectly straight and decent smile.

While much changed outwardly and physically, over time (lots and lots of time) we realized that the true character-building was in fact based on our notion of self and understanding of our "insides." (Yes, that last sentence is covered in Cheez Whiz and we're damn proud of it.)

Same goes for vegetables (not the cheese part): It's what's inside that counts. In addition to containing folate and fiber, many veggies also are chock-full of antioxidants and calcium. The introduction of a variety of vegetables into your daily diet will inevitably increase your intake of both nutrients. Each of the recipes in this chapter illustrates the ease with which you can begin this inclusion process.

Antioxidants: Guerilla Warfare

Some of these things are not like the others; some of these things are never the same: grapes, squash, soybeans, red wine, chocolate, green tea, tomatoes, pomegranates, sweet potatoes, carrots, spinach, cantaloupe, kale, watermelon, papaya, apricots, pink grapefruit, strawberries, Brazil nuts, broccoli, mangoes, and blueberries.

But they all contain antioxidants. You too occasionally pretend that you aren't related to members of your extended, and more often immediate, family. Unfortunately, you are constantly reminded that you share the same DNA. It's the same gig. The cantaloupe is not thrilled to be included at the same family reunion as the Brazil nut, but alas, they share the unique quality of being beneficial to your health.

Each of the above items is composed of substances that prevent free-radical damage. Visions of a South American guerilla regime are dancing in your head, but "free-radical damage," as it relates to nutrition and not the front page of the *New York Times*, occurs when cells are subjected to oxidation.

Oxidation occurs when a specific type of oxygen molecule destroys part of your cells. This chemically reactive oxygen causes a dominolike chain reaction, damaging even more tissue and creating more molecules like itself. Antioxidants are believed to prevent this chain reaction from occurring.

Recent research suggests that antioxidants may protect against heart disease as well as some types of cancer. Although the research is still not definitive, wouldn't you want to hedge your bet on the side of antioxidants preventing cancer and heart disease? Let's be honest, anything that might thwart the "C-word" is worth integrating in your daily routine. For slackers who avoid the real McCoy by taking "antioxidant supplements," just note that they have not been shown to have any impact on decreasing the risk of heart disease, which is why the American Heart Association recommends eating a wide variety of antioxidant-rich foods instead of taking a supplement.

Much like reading a novel, savoring each character and scene or the prose and dialogue is more satisfying than skimming the CliffsNotes; similarly, *it's always better to get antioxidants from their natural source.* By eating a varied diet based on the food-guide pyramid, at least two to three servings of fruit and four to six servings of vegetables per day, you can get your daily dose of antioxidants. Remember, different color fruits and vegetable groups provide different antioxidants, so choose a variety of both: red (tomato, watermelon), orange (pumpkin, carrot), white (cauliflower, onion), green (Romaine lettuce, spinach), and purple (eggplant, blueberries).

Sticks and Stones Will Break Your Bones, But Calcium Will Never Hurt You

Your aversion to milk began twenty-five years ago when at the end of each meal your mother demanded you "Finish your milk. The calcium will make your bones strong and help you grow up to be big and tall." Well, you're still 5'3", which means not only did your mother pull your leg, but your pediatrician lied straight to your face when he reassured you that you would hit 5'8".

You're not about to join the WNBA. You haven't grown an inch since puberty. You are forced to hem five inches off every new pair of jeans. And your white-toothed smile has been a showstopper since you had your braces removed, and the only thing growing on your body is your waistline. Why then should you be concerned with calcium consumption?

As it turns out, calcium is the fifth most abundant element in our bodies. In addition to being crucial to bone and teeth composition, calcium is involved in muscle contraction, sending messages between nerves and other cells, and releasing hormones. Calcium also aids in blood clotting, regulating how the heart works, and possibly lowering blood pressure. It can also help decrease PMS symptoms. If that's not reason enough for you to monitor your calcium intake, then perhaps this is: *Calcium is critical in preventing osteoporosis.* Now, you'll play the smarty-pants-I-received-an-A-in-biology card and launch into your mantra about how bone mass cannot be added after your twenties. True. But you still need calcium, as your bones are in a state of flux—breaking down and rebuilding. Calcium consumption is an integral aspect of this rebuilding process.

Need another reason to eat dairy? Products like low-fat yogurt and string cheese are the ideal snack because they can curb your appetite. It's the perfect combination of protein and fat that triggers your brain to think its hunger has been satiated. Thus, you eat less. Genius.

Unless you're prepared to lose a few centimeters off that 5'3" frame every decade, you might want to consider your sources of calcium intake.

- You need 1,000 milligrams (mg) or about *three* servings a day.
- One serving is equal to one of the following (*Note*: These foods are not all equal in calorie content!):
  - *8 ounces low-fat or nonfat milk*
  - *8 ounces low-fat or nonfat yogurt*
  - *⅓ cup low-fat shredded cheese*
  - *1 cup pudding (with calcium)*
  - *1 cup low-fat frozen yogurt (with calcium)*
  - *1½ to 2 cups low-fat or nonfat cottage cheese*
- The best sources of calcium from dairy:
  - *Low-fat or nonfat milk*
  - *Low-fat or nonfat yogurt*
  - *Cheese (low-fat cottage cheese, string cheese, part-skim mozzarella, and Laughing Cow cheese are perfect low-fat options)*
- Other foods rich in calcium are:
  - *Tofu*
  - *Fish with bones (sardine or salmon)*
  - *Beans*
  - *Almonds*
  - *Green vegetables like spinach, bok choy, kale, and broccoli*
- If you're lactose intolerant, there's no excuse to skimp on calcium. The following are all healthy suppliers of calcium and may be necessary if you're not eating the above sources frequently:
  - *Calcium-fortified soy milk*
  - *Lactaid milk*
  - *Orange juice (Not all OJ is calcium fortified)*
- Calcium supplements are an option but foods with calcium also often provide a wide variety of other nutrients, such as vitamin D, which is necessary for strong bones.

Sautéed Zucchini Ribbons

1. Heat a 10" (or larger) skillet over medium high heat and coat it with the olive oil. When the pan and oil are hot, add the zucchini.

2. Sauté the ribbons until slightly golden, about 1 to 2 minutes, then flip them, using tongs, and let cook an additional 1 to 3 minutes. Season with salt and pepper.

3. Remove the zucchini from the heat. Toss in the parsley and walnuts.

QUICKIES

- *Using a vegetable peeler, run the blade along the length of the zucchini. This will create thin ribbons.*

- *Toast nuts on a baking sheet in a 300°F oven for just a few minutes. They are done cooking as soon as you can smell them. Overcooking them will burn their oils and they'll become bitter. You can also toast them in a dry pan (without oil) on the stove; toss them occasionally.*

NUTRIENTS
Antioxidants
Calcium
Fiber
Folate
Omega-3

1 zucchini, cut into ribbons (It's fine to keep the skin on since it's so thin and tender.)

½ tablespoon extra-virgin olive oil

Salt and pepper to taste

1 teaspoon chopped fresh Italian flat-leaf parsley (optional)

½ tablespoon toasted walnuts, chopped

COOKING ACCESSORIES
Vegetable peeler
Chef's knife
10" (or larger) skillet
Tongs

Swiss Chard with Shallots, Raisins, and Pine Nuts

NUTRIENTS
Antioxidants
Calcium

½ bunch Swiss chard, about 2½ cups
½ tablespoon extra-virgin olive oil
1 shallot, thinly sliced
2 tablespoons raisins
⅓ cup chicken broth or stock
Salt and pepper to taste
1 teaspoon toasted pine nuts

COOKING ACCESSORIES
Chef's knife
10" Skillet with lid
Tongs

1. Cut large stems from the chard and discard. Cut the chard crosswise into 1" strips.

2. Heat a medium skillet over medium heat and coat it with the olive oil.

3. When the pan and oil are hot, add the shallots and cook until translucent, 1 to 2 minutes.

4. Add the chard, raisins, and broth or stock.

5. Cover, turn the heat to low, and cook for 10 minutes until the chard is tender. Check it once to make sure it's not burning. If the pan gets too dry, just add more chicken broth to keep it from burning and toss with tongs.

6. Season with salt and pepper and top with the pine nuts.

QUICKIES

- *Swiss chard is a member of the beet family and is a dark green leafy veggie. The stalks can be white, deep red, or all different colors if you find rainbow chard. The stalks tend to be very thick, so you should remove them since they'll take longer to cook than the leaves. It is heartier than spinach, but you can always substitute spinach if necessary.*

- *For a tip on cutting "crosswise," see page 62.*

- *Toast nuts on a baking sheet in a 300°F oven for just a few minutes. They are done cooking as soon as you can smell them. Overcooking them will burn their oils and they'll become bitter. You can also toast them in a dry pan (without oil) on the stove; toss them occasionally.*

Baby Broccoli with Sun-Dried Tomato Pesto

1. First make the pesto: Combine the tomatoes, almonds, garlic, Parmesan, lemon juice, salt, and pepper in a food processor or blender. If using already-made pesto from your freezer, let the pesto thaw prior to using it.

2. Blend until smooth, about 15 to 20 seconds.

3. Trim ends off of the broccoli.

4. Bring a pot of salted water to a boil, add the broccoli, and cook until crisp-tender, about 3 to 5 minutes. Drain well in a colander.

5. Toss the broccoli with 1 tablespoon of the pesto and mix well. Serve hot or cool.

QUICKIES

- *You can store the leftover pesto in the freezer for later use. Fill ice cube trays with the pesto, wrap in plastic, and freeze. You can keep them in the tray, or pop them out once frozen and keep them in a freezer-safe bag.*

- *For a lower-fat option, substitute sun-dried tomatoes in water, or dried ones, for the type that is packed in oil. If you use dried, soak them in ½ cup hot water for 20 minutes, then drain before using.*

- *To get rid of the scent of garlic from your hands, slice a lemon in half and rub it all over. The acid in the juice helps remove the odor.*

NUTRIENTS
Antioxidants
Calcium
Fiber
Folate

5 ounces sun-dried tomatoes, in olive oil

1 tablespoon toasted almonds

1 small clove garlic, chopped (or use a garlic press)

1 ounce grated Parmesan cheese

1 teaspoon fresh lemon juice

Salt and pepper to taste

3 ounces baby broccoli (regular broccoli will work fine, too), about 1 handful

COOKING ACCESSORIES
7" Sauté pan or nonstick baking sheet

Garlic press (optional)

Food processor or blender

Chef's knife

4-quart (or larger) pot

Colander

Brussels Sprouts with Maple Syrup and Bacon

1 large handful Brussels sprouts

1 slice bacon (freeze what you don't use)

Salt and pepper to taste

¼ cup chicken stock or canned, low-sodium chicken broth

1 tablespoon maple syrup

¼ teaspoon chopped fresh rosemary (leaves only, no stems)

¼ teaspoon chopped fresh thyme (leaves only, no stems)

COOKING ACCESSORIES

Chef's knife

7" Sauté pan with lid

Wooden spoon or heat-resistant spatula

1. Discard any wilted leaves from the Brussels sprouts, trim the root ends, and slice, lengthwise, in half. If you have some smaller ones, leave them whole.

2. Heat a sauté pan on medium heat. You don't need to add any oil in the pan because there is enough fat in the bacon to keep it from burning. Cook the bacon slice until crispy, remove it from the pan, and drain on a paper towel. Reserve the bacon fat in the pan.

3. Add the sprouts to the same pan with the remaining bacon fat, season with salt and pepper, and add the chicken broth. If the pan is too dry, add a pat of butter or more chicken broth.

4. Reduce the heat to low, cover, and let roast for 10 minutes, checking the pan occasionally to make sure it hasn't dried out.

5. Add the syrup, rosemary, and thyme and let roast for another 10 to 15 minutes, until the Brussels sprouts are tender but not mushy. If the pan gets too dry, the syrup will burn, so add a splash more chicken broth if necessary.

6. Transfer the sprouts to a plate or bowl. Crumble the bacon and scatter on top.

QUICKIES

- *Low-fat suggestion: Replace regular bacon with turkey bacon, which decreases both calories and fat content.*

- *To chop herbs, gather them up into a bundle together and chop with a chef's knife.*

Green Beans with Whole-Grain Mustard Dressing

1. Bring a pot of salted water to a boil.

2. Meanwhile, whisk together the lemon juice, olive oil, mustard, shallot, garlic, salt, and pepper vigorously for 10 seconds.

3. Add the green beans to the boiling water and cook until crisp-tender. Drain well in a colander.

4. Toss the beans in dressing and mix well. This dish can be served warm, at room temperature, or cold.

QUICKIE

- *Shallots are similar to onions but have a more delicate, sweeter flavor. You can find them in your grocery store next to onions, or sometimes near the garlic. They're perfect for meals-for-one because they are much smaller than onions.*

NUTRIENTS
Antioxidants
Calcium
Fiber
Folate

1 teaspoon lemon juice

½ tablespoon extra-virgin olive oil

1 teaspoon whole-grain mustard

1 tablespoon shallot, finely chopped

1 small garlic clove, finely chopped (or use a garlic press)

Salt and pepper to taste

¼ pound green beans, stem ends trimmed

COOKING ACCESSORIES
Chef's knife
Garlic press (optional)
Whisk
4-quart pot
Colander
Bowl

Grilled Asparagus with Fresh Lemon and Olives

NUTRIENTS
Antioxidants
Calcium
Fiber
Folate

¼ bunch asparagus, about 4 spears

½ teaspoon extra-virgin olive oil

Salt and pepper to taste

Juice of a quarter lemon

1 tablespoon roughly chopped pitted black kalamata olives

COOKING ACCESSORIES
Bowl

Grill pan or barbeque

Tongs

1. Heat the grill pan or barbecue on medium high heat.

2. To prepare the asparagus, hold one spear at each end and bend it until the end snaps off. It will snap off at the point where you need to trim off the less-desirable part of the stalk. Now return that spear to the remaining asparagus and trim them, using the one you snapped as a guide.

3. In a bowl, toss the asparagus in the olive oil, salt, and pepper.

4. Place the asparagus on the hot grill and let it cook until you can see grill marks, about 2 to 3 minutes.

5. Flip them over using tongs and finish cooking on the other side.

6. Place the grilled asparagus back in the bowl and toss with the lemon juice.

7. Scatter the chopped olives on top. This is great served hot or cold.

QUICKIE

- *The cooking time differs depending on the thickness of the asparagus. For asparagus that is about ½" in diameter, total cooking time is only about 4 to 5 minutes. It is important not to overcook it. It should still be slightly crisp and maintain a slight crunch.*

Grilled Yellow Squash and Zucchini

1. Heat the grill pan or barbecue on medium high heat.

2. With a chef's knife, trim the ends of the squash and zucchini; slice lengthwise into ½" strips.

3. Brush each side with olive oil and sprinkle with salt and pepper.

4. Grill until there are good grill marks on the squash and zucchini (the black lines left from the grill), about 2 minutes.

5. Flip the squash and zucchini with tongs and finish cooking until crisp-tender. Remove it from the grill.

6. Brush the squash and zucchini with a thin layer of balsamic vinegar and sprinkle with basil.

QUICKIE

● *Zucchini and yellow squash, sometimes called Goldbar, are best in the summer. Other varieties you can substitute are crookneck, pattypan, or even chayote.*

NUTRIENTS
Antioxidants
Calcium
Fiber
Folate

1 small yellow squash

1 small zucchini

1 teaspoon extra-virgin olive oil

Salt and pepper to taste

Drizzle of balsamic vinegar

1 tablespoon chopped fresh basil (leaves only, no stems)

COOKING ACCESSORIES
Grill pan or barbecue
Chef's knife
Brush
Tongs

Roasted Golden Beets with Goat Cheese and Hazelnuts

3 medium golden beets (regular red beets work just as well)

1 tablespoon fresh orange juice

½ tablespoon champagne vinegar

1 teaspoon chopped fresh tarragon (leaves only, no stems)

1 teaspoon chopped fresh Italian flat-leaf parsley

Pinch of salt

Pinch of pepper

1 tablespoon goat cheese

2 teaspoons roughly chopped toasted hazelnuts

COOKING ACCESSORIES

Chef's knife

Baking dish (any one from our "Pots and Pans" list, page 28)

Aluminum foil

Baking Sheet

Whisk

Bowl

1. Heat the oven to 400°F.

2. With a chef's knife, remove the beet stems and wash the beets well, being sure to wipe off any dirt.

3. Slice each beet in half and place in an oven-safe dish. Add ¼" water and cover the dish with foil.

4. Roast the beets in the oven until a knife easily slides in and out, 30 to 45 minutes depending on their size.

5. Remove beets from the oven. Once cool, peel off the skin with your fingers and discard. Slice each beet into ¼"-thick half moons.

6. In a bowl, whisk together the orange juice, champagne vinegar, tarragon, parsley, and a pinch of salt and pepper. Add the beets and mix well. Crumble the goat cheese and scatter the hazelnuts over the beets.

QUICKIES

- *Beets are root vegetables that are most commonly found in the deep red variety. Other varieties include golden beets and Chioggia beets, which are also called "candy cane" beets because of their striped red and white flesh. If you buy the whole beet, which includes the beet greens at the top of the stalk, you can remove those and cook them as you would spinach or Swiss chard.*

- *Toast nuts on a baking sheet in a 300°F oven for just a few minutes. They are done cooking as soon as you can smell them. Overcooking them will burn their oils and they'll become bitter. You can also toast them in a dry pan (without oil) on the stove; toss them occasionally.*

- *Hazelnuts are also called filberts.*

Sesame Baby Bok Choy

1. Clean the bok choy well, discarding any wilted leaves and trimming off the root.

2. Slice crosswise into 1" strips (perpendicular with the spine of the bok choy). Use both the white and green parts.

3. Heat a 10" skillet over medium high heat. Drizzle in enough peanut oil to coat the bottom of the pan.

4. When the pan is hot, add the garlic and ginger, sautéing until fragrant, about 20 seconds. Using a wooden spoon or heat-resistant spatula, take care not to burn it by stirring—turn down the heat if it starts to brown.

5. Add the bok choy, lime juice, sugar, and soy sauce and cook 2 to 3 minutes, until bok choy is crisp-tender.

6. Stir in the sesame oil and a pinch of salt.

QUICKIE

● *The best way to peel ginger is with a spoon. Yes, a spoon. Also, instead of chopping it, you can use a microplane to finely grate it.*

NUTRIENTS
Antioxidants
Calcium
Fiber
Folate

2 to 3 heads baby bok choy, depending on their size. You'll need about 2 cups once it's chopped.

1 teaspoon peanut oil or vegetable oil

½ small clove garlic, finely chopped (or use a garlic press)

1 teaspoon peeled and finely chopped fresh ginger

Juice of half a lime

½ teaspoon sugar

1 teaspoon light soy sauce

¼ teaspoon sesame oil

Pinch of salt

COOKING ACCESSORIES
Chef's knife

10" Skillet

Garlic press (optional)

Wooden spoon or heat-resistant spatula

Microplane (optional)

Sautéed Spinach

NUTRIENTS
Antioxidants
Calcium
Folate

½ tablespoon extra-virgin olive oil

1 shallot, sliced

1 tablespoon white wine

½ teaspoon fresh lemon juice

½ bag baby spinach

Salt and pepper to taste

1 teaspoon toasted pine nuts

COOKING ACCESSORIES

7" Sauté pan or nonstick baking sheet

10" Skillet

Tongs

1. Heat the olive oil in a 10" skillet over medium heat.

2. When the pan is hot, add the shallot and cook until translucent, but not brown.

3. Add the wine and cook until it evaporates.

4. Add the lemon juice and spinach and toss with tongs until the spinach wilts. It takes only a matter of seconds. Do not overcook!

5. Season with salt and pepper and sprinkle with the pine nuts.

QUICKIES

- *The flavor of wine concentrates when it cooks, so choose a wine that you won't pay an arm and a leg for. Generally you'll want a dry wine that won't impart too much sweetness into the dish. Don't waste your time with "cooking wine." It has poor flavor and is full of salt.*

- *Toast nuts on a baking sheet in a 300°F oven for just a few minutes. They are done cooking as soon as you can smell them. Overcooking them will burn their oils and they'll become bitter. You can also toast them in a dry pan (without oil) on the stove; toss them occasionally.*

Mushroom Ragout

1. In a 10" (or larger) skillet, melt the butter or pour the olive oil over medium high heat.

2. When the pan is hot, add the mushrooms and sauté for about 5 minutes, or until the mushrooms begin to soften and most of the moisture that comes out of the mushrooms evaporates.

3. Add the shallots to the mushrooms and cook until the shallots are translucent, about 2 to 3 minutes, stirring with a wooden spoon or heat-resistant spatula.

4. Add the garlic and cook until fragrant (only 10 seconds or so).

5. Add the wine and broth and scrape up any browned bits from the bottom of the pan. Let the liquids cook down and evaporate until the pan is almost dry.

6. Stir in the thyme and season with salt and pepper.

QUICKIE

- *This freezes well. To use after freezing, let thaw and then reheat on medium low heat in a small saucepan or skillet.*

- *Choose your favorite mushrooms for this. Most markets these days have a large variety of both wild and cultivated mushrooms. Wild mushrooms include chantarelle, shiitake, oyster, and porcini. Cultivated includes white button, crimini (which are baby portobellos), and portobellos.*

- *Shallots are similar to onions but have a more delicate, sweeter flavor. You can find them in your grocery store next to onions, or sometimes near the garlic. They're perfect for meals-for-one because they are much smaller than onions.*

NUTRIENTS
Antioxidants
Fiber
Folate

½ tablespoon butter or extra-virgin olive oil

3 cups assorted mushrooms, sliced into ¼" pieces

1 shallot, chopped

1 clove garlic, minced (or use a garlic press)

1 teaspoon chopped fresh thyme (leaves only, no stems)

2 tablespoons white wine (sherry or Madeira also work well with mushrooms and can be substituted in this recipe)

¼ cup low-sodium chicken broth

Salt and pepper to taste

COOKING ACCESSORIES
Chef's knife

Garlic press (optional)

10" (or larger) skillet

Wooden spoon or heat-resistant spatula

Mediterranean Eggplant

NUTRIENTS
Antioxidants
Calcium
Fiber
Folate

1 small eggplant, ends trimmed, then cut into ¼"- to ½"-thick rounds

Extra-virgin olive oil to brush on eggplant, about 1 tablespoon

Juice of half a lemon

¼ teaspoon ground cumin

Salt and pepper to taste

1 to 2 ounces good feta cheese (1 or 2 tablespoons)

1 teaspoon chopped fresh mint (leaves only, no stems)

COOKING ACCESSORIES

Chef's knife

Nonstick baking sheet

Bowl

Brush

1. Heat the oven to 400°F.

2. Place the eggplant slices on a baking sheet.

3. In a bowl, combine the olive oil, lemon juice, and cumin.

4. Brush both sides of the eggplant slices with the lemon juice mixture.

5. Sprinkle both sides of the eggplant slices with salt and pepper.

6. Roast until tender. Sprinkle the feta over each slice and cook about 2 minutes longer, until the feta begins to melt.

7. Remove the eggplant from the oven and scatter mint over the cooked slices.

QUICKIE

- *Originating in Greece, feta cheese is classically made from sheep or goat milk, but today is often made from cow milk as well. (The sheep and goat milk varieties have a superior flavor, however, so look for those.) The cheese is stored in a salty brine and has a tangy flavor. Two brands to try are Mt. Vikos or Valbreso.*

Bread-Crumb Cauliflower

1. Bring a pot of salted water to a boil.

2. Meanwhile, melt the butter in a 7" sauté pan over medium low heat.

3. Add the bread crumbs, parsley, and lemon zest to the sauté pan and stir to combine well. Cook until the bread crumbs begin to toast slightly. Remove the pan from the heat and set it aside.

4. Add the cauliflower to the boiling water and boil, about 5 minutes or until just fork-tender, not mushy. Drain in a colander.

5. Toss the cauliflower with salt, pepper, and bread crumb mixture.

QUICKIES

● *For a little something extra: Instead of following step 5, place the cooked florets into an oven-safe dish and top with the salt, pepper, and bread crumbs. Sprinkle grated Parmesan or Gruyère cheese on top and broil in the oven until the cheese bubbles and turns golden, about 2 to 3 minutes.*

● *Cauliflower florets are the clusters that sit at the top of the stems. Choose a cauliflower that has tightly packed florets and no discoloration.*

● *The easiest way to zest a lemon is to use a microplane. Just be careful to remove only the yellow part of the skin because the white pith is very bitter. If you don't have a microplane, you can peel the skin off using a vegetable peeler and finely chop it with a knife.*

NUTRIENTS
Antioxidants
Fiber
Folate

1½ cups small cauliflower florets, or large ones roughly chopped into bite-sized pieces

½ to 1 tablespoon butter

Zest from half a lemon

½ tablespoon Italian flat-leaf parsley

2 tablespoons bread crumbs (store-bought are perfectly fine)

Salt and pepper to taste

COOKING ACCESSORIES
Chef's knife
Microplane
4-quart pot
7" Sauté pan
Colander

Caramelized Onions

1 teaspoon extra-virgin olive oil

1 onion, sliced into ⅛" slices

Salt and pepper to taste

½ tablespoon balsamic vinegar

COOKING ACCESSORIES

Chef's knife

10" Skillet

Wooden spoon or heat-resistant spatula

1. Heat the oil in a 10" skillet over medium low heat.

2. When the pan is heated, add the onion, salt, and pepper. Stir together using a wooden spoon or heat-resistant spatula. Cook slowly until onions are very soft and a deep brown, stirring occasionally. This can take about 30 minutes. If you cook them too fast, the outsides will burn before the inside has a chance to cook. The longer the onions cook, the more flavor will develop.

3. Add the vinegar and cook until it evaporates.

QUICKIES

- *Carmelized onions freeze well. To use after freezing, let thaw at room temperature or in the refrigerator.*

- *Basically, any onion will do in this recipe: yellow, red, Spanish, or white. For a gourmet touch, try varieties like Vidalia, Walla Walla, Maui, or OSO Sweets.*

Sugar-Snap Peas and Edamame with Sesame-Garlic Vinaigrette

1. Bring a pot of water to a boil. Add 2 teaspoons salt.

2. Blanch the peas: Add the sugar-snap peas to boiling water and cook about 1 to 2 minutes, or until tender but still crisp. Using a slotted spoon or tongs, plunge the peas immediately into a bowl of ice water until they cool off, then drain them in a colander.

3. In a bowl combine the sesame oil, garlic, and soy sauce in a bowl

4. Add the peas and edamame and combine well.

QUICKIES

● Edamame *literally means "beans on branches" and is the Japanese word for soybean. You can find them already cooked or frozen in their pods. Follow package instructions for heating and shelling.*

● *To clean your sugar-snap peas, carefully trim the root end without cutting through completely, then pull downward to remove the stringy piece that runs down the length of the pea.*

● *Hoisin sauce is a sweet, thick sauce made from soybeans, garlic, and spices. It can be found on the Asian foods aisle of your grocery store.*

NUTRIENTS
Antioxidants
Calcium
Fiber
Folate

2 teaspoons salt

1 handful sugar-snap peas, about ⅓ cup, cleaned (do not shell)

1 handful edamame, about ⅓ cup, shelled

¼ teaspoon sesame oil

½ small clove garlic, minced (or use a garlic press)

1 teaspoon light soy sauce

1 teaspoon Hoisin sauce

COOKING ACCESSORIES
4-quart pot
Slotted spoon or tongs
Bowl for ice bath
Chef's knife or garlic press
Bowl

Miso Glazed Eggplant, Carrots, and Broccoli

NUTRIENTS
Antioxidants
Calcium
Fiber
Folate
Low-fat

½ tablespoon sweet white miso

½ tablespoon mirin

½ tablespoon rice wine vinegar

½ tablespoon honey

1 teaspoon soy sauce

1 small clove garlic, minced

½ teaspoon fresh ginger, peeled and minced

1 small Japanese eggplant, cut into ½" pieces

1 carrot, peeled and cut into ¼" pieces

½ cup small broccoli florets

Salt and pepper to taste

COOKING ACCESSORIES

Garlic press (optional)

Microplane (optional)

Whisk

Chef's knife

Vegetable peeler

Bowl

Oven-safe dish or nonstick baking sheet

1. Heat the oven to 400°F.

2. In a small bowl, combine the miso, mirin, rice vinegar, honey, soy sauce, garlic, and ginger with a whisk.

3. Toss the vegetables in the miso mixture, add salt and pepper and pour, in an even layer, into an oven-safe dish or onto a baking sheet. Cook for about 15–20 minutes, or until the veggies are tender but not mushy.

QUICKIES

- *Extra Miso Glaze can be frozen. To use again, let it thaw at room temperature or in the fridge.*

- *You can easily use any of your favorite veggies in this dish. Red peppers, mushrooms, and/or asparagus would all be delicious.*

- *Mirin is sweet Japanese cooking wine. It can be found in the Asian foods aisle of your supermarket.*

- *Miso, a flavor staple in Japan, is simply fermented soybean paste. It can be found in either the Asian foods aisle or the specialty refrigerated sections of most grocery or natural foods stores.*

- *Japanese eggplants are much narrower and have a slightly sweeter flesh than the larger, more common variety, though you can use either.*

- *The best way to peel ginger is with a spoon. Yes, a spoon. Also, instead of chopping it, you can use a microplane to finely grate it.*

North African Carrot Salad

1. Combine the oil, lemon juice, honey, and cumin in a bowl and mix well.

2. Add the cilantro, carrots, raisins, salt, and pepper. Stir well.

QUICKIES

- *This dish can be eaten immediately or can be refrigerated for a couple of days and noshed later. If you don't like cilantro, use Italian parsley instead.*

- *Cilantro looks similar to Italian parsley, and as luck would have it they're usually next to each other in the supermarket. Cilantro has relatively tender and flavorful stems, so except for the bottom inch or so, it's okay to use the stems in a food processor.*

NUTRIENTS
Antioxidants
Fiber

1 teaspoon extra-virgin olive oil

Juice of half a lemon

¼ teaspoon honey

¼ teaspoon ground cumin

½ tablespoon chopped fresh cilantro (leaves only, no stems)

2 carrots, peeled and cut on an angle into ⅛" slices

1 tablespoon golden raisins

Salt and pepper to taste

COOKING ACCESSORIES
Chef's knife
Vegetable peeler
Bowl

Voltaire

"Nothing would be more tiresome than eating and drinking if God had not made them a pleasure as well as a necessity."

CHAPTER SIX

chicken, pork, beef, seafood, and frittatas
that's a mouthful

We've all attempted being an herbivore at least once, or at least thought about it for five minutes. When push comes to shove, however, we love our protein.

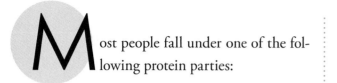

Most people fall under one of the following protein parties:

1. Have made a vow of chastity and refuse to eat any meat for the balance of our lives (we've sworn off many other things, many times: caffeine, booze, chocolate, and loser guys). The only animal products we consume are eggs. So help us God.
2. Avoid all red meats since we watched Bambi's mother get shot by the hunter. We now live a life based on white meat purity.
3. Shun all meat except for seafood, as we have an "issue" with eating animals with four legs or wings.
4. Shun all seafood, as we have an "issue" with eating animals that don't have four legs or wings.
5. Eat all meat: white, red, light, dark, with four legs, and with wings. This girl's up for anything, anytime, anywhere. So help us God.

Whatever your meat mantra, there are many redeeming attributes of proteins (including red meat). That being the case, we're going to break this all down in terms of soy, fats (unsaturated, saturated, trans fats, and fat free), cholesterol, and omega-3 and omega-6 fatty acids. In addition, given that a variety of protein preparations include the usage of salt, we're also going to walk through the CliffsNotes of the nutritional effects of sodium and how it relates to a balanced diet.

Oy Soy!

"Oy soy!" cries your newly converted macrobiotic, PETA-card-carrying friend. "It's amazing and you'll never have to eat meat again because it's a protein." While she's correct about soy being a protein, we'd like to explore this magical moment a little more before you swear off your carnivorous behavior for the balance of your life. And, if you are like the typical female, you're of the mindset that more is better. More shoes, more jewelry, more handbags, more sex, more soy. So hold off for the time being. This isn't one of those times.

Aside from commonplace foods like tofu and edamame, our Nippon-obsessed culture has been inundated with soy cookies, soy-infused protein bars, and soy chips. Although soy can be a good alternative to animal protein, as it is lower in fat and saturated fat, it is best to include it in your diet in moderation. When possible, opt for whole soy foods such as tofu, soy nuts, and miso rather than soy cookies and bars.

Concern has also been raised about the abundant use of soy in many food products. The concern with certain products (but not all) that contain soy is that they often contain soy isolates or other isolated parts of the soybean. In essence, part of the soybean has literally been "isolated" from the "whole food"; consequently, the soy in these products is in much higher concentrations than what is found naturally in tofu, soy nuts, or edamame. The concern is that soy may possibly mimic estrogen. If you're consuming higher concentrations than what's normally found in whole-soy foods, it is possible that you are exposing yourself to a significant external estrogen source. While the consequences of this are not known, there is worry as to what these high levels of hormones might be able to do. This brings us back to the fact that most foods are beneficial when eaten as a whole food, rather than eating an amino acid, vitamin, mineral, or something else extracted from that food.

Now, this is not to try to discourage you from eating soy products. If you are not a vegetarian and do not have some allergy that causes you to need to eat soy in such large quantities, you are probably best off eating soy in small quantities and from primarily whole soy foods. That means it's best to be wary of overindulging on those soy chips, protein bars, soy cookies, etc. And if you have high cholesterol, soy consumption should by no means be your *only* solution for lowering it. Consult a doctor about your specific medical regimen, but a low-fat, high-fiber diet in combination with a consistent exercise program is a great place to start.

Fatty Fatty Fatterstein: Seduced by Savory and Titillated by Sweets

If you're anything like us, you fall into one of two fat categories: *Seduced by Savory (SBS)* or *Titillated by Sweets (TBS)*. If you are innately satisfied by sweets and eating chocolate is the barometer of your happiness, then you undoubtedly belong to one of the oldest sororities on earth, TBS. Please note, we will not disclose the secret handshake or the ancient and clandestine knock of TBS. The initiation process of this selective society, however, does require the ability to inhale an entire pint of Ben & Jerry's Cherry Garcia or Half Baked ice cream in one sitting. Your secret induction took place in eighth grade on a Saturday afternoon while watching *The Real World*. Yes, those were the days when not only were you convinced that reality TV would revolutionize, not erode, the moral fabric of entertainment, but that you'd always be a size two. And, long before your tolerance for reality TV reached its breaking point, your ability to polish off a pint in the span of a thirty-minute sitcom was standard operating procedure. Your own former real world was one in which you didn't gain any weight. You're still wondering if that was the result of sheer bliss or dumb luck; either way, your carte blanche for unlimited ice cream consumption was revoked shortly thereafter.

SBS has an equally impressive history and is comprised of a dedicated sisterhood. SBS women have been known to scour the earth for the softest Camemberts, the richest Goudas, and the bluest, most pungent Stiltons. You know who you are. You're the girl who, without fail, offers your guests a smorgasbord of herbed chèvre, aged Muenster, horseradish sharp Cheddar, peppercorn salami, prosciutto, and pâté when they suddenly drop in for a glass of champagne. And while we could all try to live off cheese and salami sandwiches for the next decade, we'd be fooling ourselves if we considered them nutritious "home-cooked" meals. On numerous occasions you and the other members of your porky posse gently cajole others into

devouring creamy spreads and buttery baked brie bowls. Years of grilled cheese sandwiches, fried chicken, macaroni and cheese, Wiener schnitzel, and quesadillas defines your culinary sense of self. You have never yearned for sweets in the aftermath of a meal. On more than one debauched evening, you've been known to buy the entire bar a round of cheesy nachos topped with sour cream and guacamole.

Ah, the yesteryears, long before food labels consumed your life. *Total Saturated Fat*—huh? *Four servings equals 35 grams of fat*—what? Whether you're SBS or TBS, a complete lack of interest in fat content directly leads to utter denial. Sadly enough, you recently figured out that eating a half wheel of cheese every other day or wolfing down a pint of pleasure isn't the hottest idea going. All was peachy until one day on the cusp of spring, the warmth of an April day reminded you of those adorable linen pants you purchased last summer. You ferreted through the depths of your closet and found them— jackpot. Perfectly dry-cleaned from the last time you wore them in early September. Only after you sucked in your gut, to the detriment of your lungs, were you able to button them. Your Buddha belly protruded over the top while your love handles slipped over the sides: the muffin top. Barely able to breathe, you clumsily waddled to the mirror. It was precisely at this moment that you reconsidered your notion of fat: which fats lead to the growth of muffin tops and which fats you need to survive. Still, you are positive your life will cease to exist if you are forced to deprive yourself of all cheeses and/or ice creams.

Fear not—fat is a very important part of a healthy diet and it gets a bad rap (mostly because we point fingers at it when our Buddha bellies refuse to fit into our pants). While it increases the flavor of food, which results in ridiculously satisfying meals, fat also has attributes that are important for your health. In addition to providing your body with energy, the molecular structure of fat allows it to transport fat-soluble vitamins in the body, which means that without fat in your diet, you wouldn't be able to absorb vitamins A, D, E, or K—no matter how much of them you took in a vitamin or ate in food. These vitamins are essential to your health and many functions in your body—think healthy skin and strong bones and so much more.

Have we jogged your memory? Are you having flashbacks to high school biology? Without fat intake, you would have no energy, you'd feel cold all the time, and you'd never get your period (that's not a good thing, despite what you may think), which means you would not be able to get pregnant. Fat in the diet is essential for normal growth and development, for keeping your hair shiny and from falling out, keeping skin healthy, preventing food cravings, protecting your organs from damage, providing essential fatty acids and, as we've already mentioned, absorbing fat-soluble vitamins. And that's just to name a few functions. Talk about a beast of burden.

This is not the time to reinstitute former eating habits and implement a diet based on nothing but chocolate croissants, flautas, coconut macaroons, and chicken katsu. There are a few caveats about fat consumption that will make you reconsider this no-holds-bar approach. Heart disease is the number-one killer of women and the risk factors include high cholesterol and obesity, which can be caused by excessive fat consumption. (Other risk factors include high blood pressure, smoking, diabetes, physical inactivity, and family history. While you may not be able to control all of these risk factors, you can definitely learn how to control many of them by reading on.) One thing you can do is eat *better* fat. For our purposes, we'll put fat in two camps: *good* (unsaturated fats: monounsaturated and polyunsaturated) and *bad* (saturated and trans fats). The fat content on the nutritional label of that Jif peanut butter just became a whole lot more meaningful.

We're guessing that you understand the basic principles of good versus evil, and that, therefore, the majority of the fat in a healthy diet should come from *unsaturated* fats. Brilliant—your arteries will thank you. We'll spare you the organic chemistry lesson and get straight to the point. The attributes that differentiate unsaturated fats from saturated and trans fats are as follows:

Unsaturated Fats (Monounsaturated and Polyunsaturated)

Unsaturated fats lower bad and total cholesterol and some can also increase good cholesterol. These fats provide your essential fatty acids

---

Fat Intake Guidelines for Your Waistline

It's also important to limit your fat intake to less than 30 percent of your total calories. For someone eating a 2,000-calorie diet, that means consuming fewer than 65 grams of fat each day. One should also limit saturated fat intake to 10 percent of the total calories or one-third of the fat calories, or about 22 grams—beware especially if cheese is your weakness in life.

(omega-3 and omega-6, page 101), which are critical to a healthy diet.

Unsaturated fats are derived primarily from plant sources and are usually liquid at room temperature. Examples include canola oil, olive oil, and vegetable oil (coconut and palm oil are the exception—they are unhealthy oils). Does this justify a two-week Greek Isle vacation under the guise of sampling life-enhancing olive oil? See if your health-insurance provider will pick up the tab, as it would most likely save them a ton of cash over the years. Unsaturated fats are also found in fish, with fatty fish such as tuna, salmon, and sardines being some of the best sources. They are also found in nuts, avocados, and olives.

Saturated Fats

Saturated fats increase your bad and total cholesterol levels, which in turn increases your risk of heart disease. Saturated fat is usually solid at room temperature and is found primarily in foods of animal origin with the exception of fish (see above). Sure as your love handles exist, you might as well duct-tape butter, bacon, lard, whole milk, cheese, and French fries to your waist. Now, the next time your grandmother whips out the five blocks of butter to bake those chunky chocolate chip cookies, you'll know why your belt loop expands by one hole the next day. And you thought it was a result of spending too much time with your immediate family.

Trans Fats

Trans fats, also known as partially hydrogenated oils, are typically found in fried foods and in packaged foods such as cookies, chips, and doughnuts because they increase shelf life. Twinkies, anyone?

Trans fats have been found to increase bad cholesterol and therefore increase the risk of heart disease. Although no safe amount has been set, many companies have started eliminating trans fats from their production. Along with banning smoking in restaurants, cities across the country are eliminating trans fats from eating establishments. Funny, explaining how we consumed trans fats and cigarette smoke in our daily lives will be much like explaining our mixed tape collection to our future children—distant memories from a world they won't understand.

In fact, beginning in January 2006, food manufacturers were required to list the amount of trans fat found in their products. But here's the kicker. Leave it to the lawyers and politicians to create a loophole by creating food-labeling laws that say that manufacturers can claim

Good (Unsaturated) Fats vs. Bad (Saturated and Trans) Fats

Good Fats	Bad Fats
Olive oil	Butter
Canola oil	Margarine
Trans-fat-free spreads	Palm oil
Peanuts	Coconut oil
Tree nuts (almonds,	Red meat
cashews, pecans, walnuts,	Lard
Brazil nuts, pistachios,	Chips
hazelnuts, pine nuts, and	French fries
macadamia nuts)	Packaged cookies
Peanut butter	Cheese
Avocado	Fried foods
Olives	Cream cheese
Mayonnaise*	Doughnuts
Salad dressing*	Ice cream
Soybean oil	Packaged cakes
Corn oil	Bacon
Sunflower oil	
Salmon	
Tuna	
Herring	

Mayo and salad dressing are healthy fat, but, as with all fats, portion size is key. Even good fats can become unhealthy if you're eating them in large quantities. Too much fat is too much.

0 grams of trans fat even if there is almost half a gram per serving. Given certain investigation, you may discover partially hydrogenated oil listed in the ingredients even though the food label fails to disclose trans fat. Beware, if you are a packaged-food junkie, because those trans fat grams add up. (And remember what we said about those serving sizes accumulating to be more than your daily allowance.) Eat a sleeve of cookies or a few too many handfuls of chips and that <0.5 gram of trans fat could translate to several grams.

Fat-Free Follies Foiled

The strategic response seems painfully obvious: Eat only fat-free food. Now you've done it; you've circumvented the system; you've outsmarted the foundation of nutritional thought; you've out foxed the fox. It's only a matter of time until you've decreased your fat intake to 0 percent. Parading around, you begin to promote a life sans fat by gorging yourself on fat-free pretzels, fat-free frozen yogurt, fat-free English muffins with fat-free turkey slices, fat-free cheese on fat-free French bread, and SnackWells. Those delicious little morsels of gluttonous-free pleasure are the apex of your fat-free existence. You pride yourself on your ability to inhale an entire

Examples of Healthy Fat Intake Redux

If you need **1,800 calories per day** instead of 1,600 calories, you have the luxury of being able to add a little more fat to your diet. Remember to choose fat from primarily healthy sources—add some olives, canola oil, and sunflower seeds to your diet—rather than loading up on butter, pastries, and sausage. For a woman eating an 1,800-calorie-per-day diet, less than 30 percent of calories should come from fat, or less than 540 daily calories. Since each gram of fat has 9 calories, one should consume 40 to 60 fat grams each day.

Additional serving sizes of fat

Grams of fat	Food
4–5	Teaspoon oil
4–6	Tablespoon nuts
5	Teaspoon mayo
5	Tablespoon regular dressing
5	Teaspoon butter or margarine
5	8–10 small olives

SAMPLE DAY'S FAT INTAKE

Food	Grams of Fat (g)
BREAKFAST	
1 cup Total Raisin Bran cereal	1
1 cup 1% milk	2
½ cup blueberries	0
LUNCH	
Chicken salad made with 1 tablespoon reduced fat mayo	5
½ cup grapes and ½ cup arugula in chicken salad	0
2 slices whole-wheat bread	2
1 Dove dark chocolate square	2.5
AFTERNOON SNACK	
1 ounce almonds	14
1 tablespoon low-fat granola	0.5
6 ounces nonfat Greek yogurt	0
DINNER	
Salad with 1 tablespoon salad dressing (e.g., Whole-Grain Mustard Dressing)	5
⅛ cup sliced avocado	4
6 small black olives	2
4 ounces grilled salmon	4
1 cup cooked spinach	0
1 teaspoon olive oil to sauté spinach	4.5
½ cup wild rice	0
DESSERT	
½ cup light ice cream	4
Total	**50.5**

box in one day. Dessert for breakfast, dessert for lunch, dessert for dinner. Weeks of guiltless consumption pass and you're flabbergasted by the fact that you've shed not a single pound. Conversely, you think you might have packed on a few L-Bs. But how could your waistline be increasing when your life is lived without sin?

Calories. Yup, that's what all of those fat-free meals amounted to: copious amounts of calories. It seems as if the unlimited quantity of SnackWell calories botched your plans for a fat-free pedigree. *But, but, but, the box said fat-free.* Sadly enough, just like your mother reminded you every time you weren't selected as the lead in the school play despite your unparalleled acting ability, *life isn't fair.* It seems as if the majority of fat-free foods counteract the lack of taste with none other than the devil itself: sugar. Consequently, these tasteless culprits are also extremely *unsatisfying* due to their lack of fat. Back to your grandmother's patented chocolate chip cookies; you are easily satiated by just one. Yes, you could eat the entire batch, but your appetite is satisfied after one.

Your willpower is an entirely different subject matter. It's not just your grandmother's cookies. The same goes for real, buttery-rich ice cream; one bowl and your appetite has cli-maxed, peaked to sweet perfection, and you're happy. In complete contrast, each time you have an extra-large fat-free frozen yogurt, you anticipate your next meal twenty minutes after you've scooped the last bite. What those frozen-yogurt shops fail to disclose is that a half cup of most *real* ice cream has only 150 calories (sadly this does not include Ben & Jerry's or Häagen Dazs with loads of cookie dough and candy schmutz). In most cases, the extra-large bowl of frozen yogurt probably has double the calories because of the sugar. Unequivocally, these extra, unused calories result in your body's perpetual ability to increase its arsenal of *fat.*

Not all low-fat and reduced-fat foods will expand your waistline. Eating them in unlimited quantities, however, will inevitably result in weight gain. Proceed with caution, as "reduced" merely means that the food has 25 percent less of that nutrient than the original product. This is not to imply that you should buy the regular version, but don't assume that because it's reduced fat you can eat as much as you want. While ice cream and cookies have unhealthy fat, limited portions are many times better for you in the long run than their fat-free cousins (with the slight exception of skim milk, which is always your best bet). And remember, some foods, such as most fruits and vegetables, are naturally fat-free. Hello, genius.

The Numbers Never Lie

Given your family history of high cholesterol and heart disease, you've decided it's about time you have your cholesterol checked. We're giving you the benefit of the doubt that (a) you know what cholesterol is and (b) you understand why it's imperative you have it checked. If you hesitated on either (a) or (b), you should probably make an appointment sooner rather than later. Yes, that means next week. Whether it's done to appease your mother or us, you'll be thankful you saddled up and discovered your lucky number. This lucky number as it relates to your arteries has nothing to do with how to find the man with whom you are the most astrologically matched. Adding your birthday with the total number of men you've kissed divided by the number of apartments you've lived in and subtracted by the number of handbags you bought last year will not help you out either.

Cholesterol happens to be one of the unsexiest things going. However, it's just as important as Fashion Week, Neiman Marcus's annual Last Call sale, and Barney's one-day-only shoe sale (which of course we think should be considered a national holiday). It is affected by genetics, lifestyle, diet, and weight, and if left to its own unruly devices, it will put you at risk for heart disease, strokes, and heart attacks. If you are wholeheartedly against tattooing the following on your body, then we hope you memorize it as best you can.

Cholesterol Superstar

Type	Optimal level
GOOD Cholesterol = HDL (High Density Lipoproteins)	Goal > 50
BAD Cholesterol = LDL (Low Density Lipoproteins)	Goal < 100
TOTAL Cholesterol	Goal < 200

As luck would have it for mnemonic lovers everywhere, you want your *LDLs to be LOW* and your *HDLs to be HIGH*. By now you're racking a mental tally of how many pastries you have consumed in your lifetime. The French Gross Domestic Product over the years has been heavily subsidized by your chocolate croissant consumption, which by all accounts means your arteries are about as clogged as your pores when you fail to have them cleansed weekly with seaweed-infused facial peels. It's a cholesterol fiasco—your personal Exxon Valdez wasteland of potential cardiac arrest.

Oddly enough, however, cholesterol has absolutely nothing to do with your dress size. You could be a size two and yet have catastrophically high cholesterol levels. If you've prided yourself on your ability to eat anything that isn't tied down, all while maintaining a Parisian runway model stature, it's time you realize that your arteries may be in dire straits. Cholesterol, which is also made naturally by your body, adheres itself to artery walls, thereby narrowing them (a condition also referred to as atherosclerosis). Typically, arteries are flexible, allowing blood to flow at its leisure. Cholesterol, much like territorial male behavior, narrows arteries and thus, increases their rigidity. Think back to the last soiree you attended where you were desperately attempting to catch a certain someone's attention, but his best friend intercepted you, chatting your ear off about last night's *Sport Center* highlights for the better part of the evening, thus making it impossible for you to beeline it to the best friend you wanted. Same thing. Cholesterol clogs the artery, making it difficult for blood to flow, thereby putting it as the leading cause of heart disease, heart attacks, and strokes.

By now, we're sure you've deduced that certain foods increase cholesterol levels, while others decrease levels. Again, the foods listed on page 95 outline which foods benefit your cholesterol and which negatively impact your health. Instituting a diet that focuses on replacing saturated and trans fats with healthier monounsaturated and polyunsaturated fats, as well as foods that include high levels of soluble fiber (see page 45), will help lower LDL and total cholesterol.

Aside from decreasing LDL and total cholesterol levels, we can also improve our heart health by increasing our HDL levels. This can be done by eating foods rich in omega-6 fatty acids, such as seeds, vegetable oil, and salad dressing (most salad dressings are made with oils rich in omega-6 fatty acids, but beware of portion sizes, as the calories and fat really add up). Perhaps the greatest breakthrough in medical research led to the concept that drinking alcohol in moderation has also been shown to increase HDL levels. We knew there was a God! (We'll chat about this favorite subject of ours in just a bit, so hold tight.) In addition to believing in higher powers that encourage our glass-of-wine-per-day prescription, the following guidelines are a few other measures for lowering your LDLs and increasing your HDLs.

- Be selective and choose the right fats by replacing saturated and trans fats with mono-unsaturated and polyunsaturated fats. Check labels if you're not sure.

- Replace your morning cubicle snack of a Krispy Kreme glaze doughnut with a handful of almonds. Switch your afternoon tide-me-over of chips and dip for 1 tablespoon peanut butter on a banana.

- Use vegetable oils (except coconut and palm kernel oils) in your cooking. This will invariably result in healthier meals and consequently cleaner arteries. Remember to use them in moderation, as fat is still high in calories—too much "healthy" fat is not good for you, either.

- Broaden your horizons and consider fish. Most fish are lower in saturated fat than meat and contain omega-3s, which are invaluable to your health (refer to the next section).

- In restaurants, ask for dressings on the side. They are usually very high in fat—and remember, too much healthy fat is not good for you, either. Here's a tip: Dip your fork into the dressing, and then into your salad.

The Ultimate Multitasker: Omega-3 Fatty Acids

Most fabulous and single girls are constantly accused of "burning the candle at both ends." It's a character flaw our mothers have charged us with since our first sleepover in second grade. You're positive that phrase will eventually head your arsenal of threatening one-liners used against your own children. However, we're fairly confident that you've failed to break the habit. Just last weekend your itinerary was booked solid. When Sunday evening rolled around, you were desperate for just *one* day of leisure. You're not sure how two days spun into oblivion, but you're certain the beginning of your demise commenced Friday afternoon, around 1:30 P.M.

Unable to concentrate on the client memo due yesterday, your mind flooded with visions of cocktail hour (you knew it was Miller Time somewhere in the world). Rallying the troops with a persuasive e-mail, you encouraged them to congregate at the nearest watering hole and join you in an evening enhanced by debauchery. So began your weekend tailspin. You relished the evening to its fullest until approximately 12:30 A.M. when you remembered your college roommate's wedding shower began at 11 A.M. the next morning. Knowing full well that a Class Five Headache awaited you at sunrise, you immediately exited stage left.

Our Average Morning After: Two Aleves, a liter of water, and a cup of thick sludge coffee later, you shower (holding the wall for stability), apply makeup (painting your face by numbers), and dress (praying that none of your friends notice that you wore the same outfit to brunch last weekend). Aside from the fact that you think you might die of dehydration given that your brain is slowly but surely detaching from your skull, you make it out of your apartment. On your way to this most perfunctory of wedding showers, your mind wanders into a dark and twisted thought. Most of us have been there, one too many times. You are desperate to be horizontal and alone in a dark room with a cold washcloth over your eyes for the next ten hours.

Seven cucumber sandwiches, five Arnold Palmers, two emergency exits to Aunt May's powder room (yes, the toilet seat was covered in a pink plastic cushion), and three too many shower games later, your afternoon was a nightmare wrapped in pastel floral wrapping paper. Somehow you survived. Arriving home later that afternoon, you are reminded that you committed to meeting high school friends for dinner that evening. Moreover, you have family brunch Sunday morning to celebrate your sister's new boyfriend's birthday. Your weekend is shot. Your plans to alphabetize your spices are obliterated. However, you still manage to clean your apartment, wash your three weeks' worth of dirty laundry, discuss your other sister's latest breakup for two hours convincing her that she deserves better, and most importantly, attend yet another wedding shower. You crawl into bed Sunday night, exhausted from your two days.

Right there with you in the realm of amazing multitaskers are omega-3 fatty acids. Who, or shall we say what, are omega-3 fatty acids? More important, why are they a member of your exclusive multitasking country club? Here's why. Omega-3s are polyunsaturated fats, which, if you've been paying attention, you know are essential in our diets. Omega-3 fats are only found in food (meaning your body doesn't produce them). Thus, it's critical to maintain a diet high in the following three types of omega-3 fatty acids: α-linolenic acid (ALA), eicosapentaenoic acid (EPA), and docosahexaenoic acid (DHA). You thought washing your laundry and attending a wedding shower hung over was difficult, but omega-3s undertake the following each day:

- Decreasing inflammation
- Decreasing triglyceride levels
- Decreasing blood pressure
- Decreasing formation of buildup in the arteries
- Decreasing the formation of blood clots
- Improving mood

In addition to curbing the average girl's mood swings, omega-3s are believed to be useful in treating and possibly preventing many chronic diseases, particularly high cholesterol, heart disease, and stroke. Just when you thought your triple major in Japanese, Chemical Engineering, and Art History from a top-ten university was impressive, omega-3 fatty acids one-upped you. They are also thought to be of benefit in the treatment of other illnesses such as:

Asthma	Dry eyes
Arthritis	High blood pressure
Cancer	Macular degeneration
Diabetes	Migraines

Ongoing research is also looking into other uses of omega-3 fatty acids such as treating depression and ulcerative colitis.

If your family history doesn't include one of the diseases mentioned above, you are more than welcome to disregard the balance of this chapter. (If you haven't already begun leveraging your disease-free genes to persuade eligible bachelors seeking future procreation, plan accordingly.) However, if you hail from genetic makeups similar to ours, take note. It's better late than never to begin integrating omega-3s into your diet. Chances are one of your grandparents and perhaps parents had/has one or more of the diseases listed. Which tells you, if you subscribe to that whole notion of genetics, that you'll stand to improve your chances by incorporating a few of the following fabulous sources of omega-3s into your daily diet:

Sardines	Omega-3 enriched eggs
Herring	Canola oil
Trout	Walnuts
Salmon	Wheat germ
Tuna	Soybeans
Mackerel	Soybean oil
Mussels	Flaxseeds
Snapper	Flaxseed oil

If you are one of the many women who avoid fish as much as you avoid cleaning your bathroom, you just threw up a little. Chances are you've been avoiding fish since childhood, given your mother's propensity to prepare a "fishlike" substance resembling something you once saw on an aquarium fieldtrip. You are convinced that you loathe fish and will avoid it for the duration of your life. You have gone so far as to inform those who offer you fish that you are in fact allergic to seafood. You don't even know how the fib slips out, but somewhere between the deep-fried fish-sticks and the Ahi tuna sashimi platter, you lie.

Here's the truth: Good fish, delicious fish, amazing fish, should not taste fishy. When you are prepared to embark on the journey across the wide world known as seafood, you'll know you have arrived, as seafood is one of life's most amazing culinary experiences and is impossibly decadent. Keep repeating: *I'm not really allergic.* Fish, as a whole, are incredible sources of omega-3s. Many government resources, including the American Heart Association, recommend eating about 6 ounces of fish per week. If you are unwilling to try new things in life or for any other reason refuse to incorporate fish into your diet, you should at least consume 2

> ### Not All Fish Have Equal Amounts of Mercury
> *Salmon, being the unpopular kid on the ocean playground, is the fish everyone talks about with regard to mercury. In actuality, the culprits that contain the highest levels are shark, mackerel, tilefish, and swordfish. It's okay to eat tuna as long as you limit it to about 6 ounces per week. Chunk light tuna is lower in mercury than other canned tuna. For more choices, check out* www.oceansalive.org.

to 3 servings of omega-3 fatty acid–rich foods each week.

The fishy kicker: mercury. There's a lot of concern about eating fish because of the high levels of mercury in it. Mercury is very toxic—long-term exposure can cause damage to the brain, kidneys, and other organs. It may also be linked to a variety of other chronic illnesses. A particular concern for females of childbearing age is that high levels of mercury can cause birth defects. The concern surrounding these levels, however, is akin to not driving because you might get into a car accident or not getting married because you might get divorced. While certain fish contain higher levels of mercury, many fish do not.

Avoiding fish because of *potential* mercury levels is counteracted by all of fish's incredible health attributes, as found in a 2006 study out of Harvard University. Translation: You should not sacrifice one of the best sources of omega-3 fatty acids by boycotting fish.

Kappa Kappa Omega-6s: The Other Sister

Omega-6s, known as linoleic acid, are also an essential fatty acid. Like omega-3s, they aid in lowering cholesterol and preventing heart disease. The optimal balance is a ratio of 4 (or less):1, omega-6 to omega-3, meaning that for every *four (or less)* omega-6 fatty acids you should have *one* omega-3 fatty acid. In the United States, however, most people have a ratio of at least 10:1. While omega-6s are just as critical in preventing the diseases we listed for omega-3s, ironically, this imbalanced ratio potentially leads to increased heart disease and depression.

One of the reasons for this imbalance is the overwhelming consumption of packaged foods. Omega-6s are found in vegetable oils, which are highly concentrated in baked and processed goods. The only way to improve your omega-6 to omega-3 ratio is with the following measures:

(1) Decrease the amount of fried foods and packaged goods you consume (cookies, crackers, snacks, and other pastries); (2) Increase your intake of omega-3-rich foods such as fish, nuts, and good oils, as mentioned above.

Sodium: Salt in the Wound

Many of us have that best guy friend. Depending on how long you've known him, you might have even introduced him to the woman he married. Given that you've provided him with a lifetime of sex, many times he's forced to listen to your ridiculous antics at 10:00 on Sunday mornings. Most of us have been there—explaining that we're still renting our studio apartments with pinkish brown carpet in the ghetto, still not married, still considering quitting our jobs, and still contemplating moving to India to become a yoga instructor. Meanwhile, he (the friend who has yet to return the favor of introducing you to your husband . . .) loves his new medical rotation in surgery. His beautiful wife loves her career as a defense attorney. And they've just purchased the most lovely three-bedroom house. Life is good.

Just when you thought you'd hit your threshold of bliss, he spilled the beans. Two of your mutual friends just proposed to their girlfriends. After talking yourself out of pulling a Sylvia Plath and crawling into the oven, you regained your composure. You were doing fine with the other weddings. However, these two newly engaged individuals are *boys*. You refuse to refer to them as men, as it is inconceivable they know *how* to get married—or that they had the wherewithal to buy a ring, not to mention find a woman to marry. You started crunching the numbers and realized that most of your guy friends from high school and college are hitched. And the timing of it all seems strangely suspicious. They all tended to propose within a month of one another. It's as if proposing is contagious. You have eight weddings scheduled in the next twelve months and your year is beginning to resemble Cupid's calendar of love. Your bank statements reflect thousands of dollars of plane tickets and Williams-Sonoma gift registry items. Not fazed, you putter along in your existence. It's all just salt in the wound.

With this said, we've decided to put a little flavor in our lives, from salt in our wounds to salt in our meals. Although the two words, salt and sodium, are often used interchangeably, they are two distinct entities. Being the bearer of savor and taste, salt is actually made of sodium (Na) and chlorine (Cl) which results

in (NaCl), or table salt. If you skipped the Periodic Table lectures in chemistry and failed to comprehend the basics on the elements, here's a quick refresher. Just as water is a combination of two elements, so is salt. The cold and refreshing beverage is a combination of two hydrogen (H) atoms and one oxygen (O) atom, hence H_2O. So while you would no sooner refer to water as hydrogen, the same applies to referring to salt as sodium.

Salt consumption directly affects one's sodium intake because it's 40 percent sodium. Sodium, and consequentially salt, live a bipolar life and often find themselves in a PR nightmare as intense as Michael Jackson's and Tom Cruise's (both of whom are salty dogs in their own right). On one altruistic hand, sodium, in small amounts, helps with many functions in the body and is crucial to a healthy diet; it maintains fluid balance, transmits nerve impulses, and maintains function of the muscles. On the opposing hand, however, a diet with too much sodium is linked to high blood pressure, or hypertension. And while approximately one in three adults suffers from high blood pressure, around a third of these individuals do not know it, because high blood pressure has no symptoms. It is critical, therefore, to have your blood pressure checked to monitor this silent killer that can lead to a heart attack, heart failure, stroke, or kidney failure.

Some people are more sensitive to sodium than others, which increases their risk of developing high blood pressure. Because family history and the risk of high blood pressure varies by individual, many nutritional organizations, including the USDA, recommend that all individuals watch their sodium intake even if they aren't sodium sensitive. Whether sensitive to sodium or not, a high-sodium diet can lead to water retention, which makes you look and feel bloated. And who needs to look bloated? The daily recommendation of sodium is a maximum of between 2,300 and 2,400 mg per day, which is the equivalent of about 1 teaspoon of salt. Only confirming your blood pressure will give you the resources to decide what amount of sodium is suited for your body.

By monitoring your salt intake you'll be able to decrease the amount of sodium you ingest each day. There are a handful of tactics you can incorporate into your daily routine to accomplish this. Introducing the following foods into your diet, as they typically contain less sodium, is one way to start. In addition, because many of these foods have not been processed, they contain a multitude of other nutrients and minerals that can be helpful in lowering blood pressure.

- Fresh fruits and vegetables
- Whole grains such as whole-wheat bread, whole-wheat pasta, and brown rice
- Low-fat or nonfat dairy such as milk, yogurt, and cheese (except cottage cheese)
- Unsalted nuts and seeds
- Beans
- Lean meat, poultry, and fish
- Foods that say "low-salt," "low-sodium," or "no salt added"

In tandem with expanding your repertoire of sodium-healthy foods, there are also a handful of measures that will reduce your sodium intake:

- Take the salt shaker off the table.
- Replace salt and instead cook with fresh herbs, spices, garlic, and onions (this will create richer and fuller flavor).
- Avoid seasonings with a lot of sodium, such as Accent and Adobo.
- Rinse canned foods (e.g., canned beans) before eating them.

- Limit your consumption of:
  - Packaged foods such as chips, pretzels, and crackers
  - Packaged soup cups and bouillon cubes
  - Fast food
  - Soy sauce, teriyaki sauce, steak sauce, ketchup, barbecue sauce
  - Cured meats such as bacon, sausage, ham, and cold cuts
  - Salted butter and margarine
  - Prepared frozen dinners
  - Pickled foods such as olives and pickles

Another way to decrease sodium consumption is by reading food labels and familiarizing yourself with their contents. Given sodium's preservative attributes, many packaged foods include large amounts to keep foods fresher longer. Even foods that mask their saltiness can include a significant amount of sodium, so beware. It's always best to eat foods that contain less than 140 mg of sodium per serving.

Also note that there are other ways to lower blood pressure besides limiting sodium intake—one of the best ways is through exercise.

Now that you've got sodium figured out, you're a bit weary on how to differentiate among the various types of salt on aisle seven in the grocery store. Given its ubiquitous nature, you're still not positive how salt ends up in those funky blue cylindrical containers with their little metal spouts. Here's how. Salt is produced by two methods: extracted from seawater through an evaporation process or harvested from salt deposits left over from ancient oceans. Salt is also available in two forms: fine-grain (iodized salt, table salt, pickling salt, popcorn salt, and sea salt) and coarse (kosher salt, rock salt, and sea salt). These salt varieties create a spectrum of textures and are derived from various locations, therefore the boldness and complexity of their flavors differ. Listed below in no particular order are the most commonly used cooking salts. And yes, they each feel the same when poured into a wound.

Iodized salt (AKA table salt): In 1924, salt had the honorary privilege of being the first fortified food by having iodine added to its composition. Now you're grossed out, as the last time you used iodine was to prevent infection on a scraped knee. However, the reason for adding iodine to salt was to create a food distribution channel that aided in the prevention of goiter. Iodized salt is typically found on your dining room table in your grandmother's pewter salt shaker.

Sea salt: Remember as a child how your eyes stung relentlessly each time you came home from the beach? Your mom always told you not to open your eyes under water, but did you listen? No. The ocean, if you hadn't received the memo, contains a substance we like to refer to as salt. Sea salt is a pure salt with no additives and is available in both fine-grain and larger coarse crystals. Because of its natural production method and milder flavor, it's the hero of salts among chefs.

Kosher salt: Ironically "kosher" salt's name is not a result of being prepared to conform to Jewish food laws; rather its name derives from the way it is used to prepare kosher meat. Due to kosher salt's organic crystal structure and larger surface area, it's perfect for absorbing moisture and curing meats. In the case of preparing kosher meat, because the Torah prohibits the consumption of any blood, kosher salt is ideal for removing the final traces of blood from meat. Kosher salt typically contains no additives and has a distinct flavor that differs from table salt. Chefs prefer its milder flavor for cooking as it's less potent and doesn't overpower the natural flavors of the food.

Funny, It Tastes like Chicken
PAGES 112–20

Chicken is cooked through when it reaches 165°F, but you should actually stop cooking it at 160°F because residual heat will bring it up to 165°F. Let the chicken "rest" for about 10 minutes before slicing, otherwise the juices will run out and leave you with a dry piece of meat. If using a thermometer, insert it into the thickest part of the meat, and make sure it doesn't touch a bone or the read will be inaccurate.

Pork: The Other White Meat
PAGES 121–25

Say what you will, but the "other white meat" has way more pull than Britney Spears. Pork is actually done cooking at 145°F, unlike the recommended 155°F. Stop cooking pork at 140°F because residual heat will bring the temperature to 145°F. It is important to let the meat "rest" for about 10 minutes before slicing, otherwise the juices will run out and you'll be stuck with a parched piece of pork. If you're using a thermometer, insert it into the thickest part of the meat—don't let it touch the bone or the read will be inaccurate.

Beef: It's What's for Dinner
PAGES 126–29

When you're choosing beef, look for meat that's an even, bright red color and that doesn't exude an odor. The highest grades of beef are Select, Choice, and Prime (select being the least expensive and prime being the most expensive). While we know you're saving for that next pair of shoes, we'd recommend choosing one of these three grades and forgo penny-pinching when it comes to your beef selection. When you cook beef, stop cooking it 5 degrees before your desired doneness (see below) because residual heat will bring it up to the right temperature. It is important to let the meat "rest" for about 10 minutes before slicing, otherwise the juices will run out and you'll be left with a leathery-looking piece of meat that you could polish your shoes with.

Degrees of Doneness

Rare . . . . *125°–130°F*
Medium Rare . . . . *130°–135°F*
  (most flavorful at this temperature)
Medium . . . . *135°–140°F*
Medium Well . . . .*140°–145°F*
Well . . . . *145°F*

Seafood: These Aren't Your Mother's Fish Sticks

PAGES 130–39

We've already mentioned the nutritional benefits of fish and are confident you'll soon be a seafood convert. Therefore, here are a few tips on what to look for when you purchase the ingredients for your next nautical-inspired meal. It doesn't have to taste fishy. Trust us. When buying fish look for the following:

- The flesh should be resilient to the touch.
- There should be no fishy odor, but the fish or shellfish should smell like the sea.
- When buying already-cut fillets, make sure none of the edges are dry and the fillet looks plump and hydrated.

Frittata-Mama: You'll Never Think of Eggs the Same Way

PAGES 140–45

Where do we begin? We love them. We want them. We need them. Perhaps it's because they're a comfort food that reminds us of our early childhood days when we were "allowed" not only to have them for dinner but to eat in front of the TV. Typically it was when our mothers were out of town and eggs were the only thing our fathers knew how to cook—the family (sans mom) sitting around watching *Cosby* reruns and having omelets with everything in the refrigerator (corn, bacon, spinach, cheese, etc.). While most of our fathers weren't the original Mr. Marthas, they were certainly on to something when it came to making eggs.

Frittatas are the grownup version of scrambled eggs. They are a hybrid of a quiche (same shape, no crust) and an omelet. Much like the puggle, the labradoodle, or the chug—designer mutts and designer eggs—they are made of a hodgepodge of ingredients that make them all the more fantastic, so master this technique. We promise, you'll be the apple of your father's eye when he finds out you've taken his mastery of eggs to a whole new level. Frittatas are perfect for any time of day: a simple breakfast, an elegant lunch, or the ultimate healthy dinner when accompanied by a salad.

Whole Roasted Chicken

NUTRIENTS
Antioxidants

1 whole chicken, about 5 pounds, rinsed and patted dry with paper towels inside and out

2 tablespoons salt

Pepper to taste

½ lemon, cut into wedges

10 cloves garlic, smashed with the side of a knife and peeled

20 sprigs (stems with the leaves on) fresh thyme, about half a bunch

1 tablespoon extra-virgin olive oil (to coat the chicken)

COOKING ACCESSORIES

Chef's knife

Kitchen string

Roasting pan or 9" × 13" baking pan with a rack

Instant-read thermometer

1. Heat the oven to 450°F.

2. Liberally season the inside of the chicken with 1 tablespoon of the salt and pepper, then stuff with the lemon, garlic, and thyme.

3. Using kitchen string, tie the legs together tightly. This ensures the chicken is compact and will cook evenly. Also, to prevent the wing tips from burning, tuck them behind the body. (If the wings were arms, this would look like a person putting her hands behind her head.)

4. Coat the outside of the chicken with the olive oil and season liberally with the remaining salt and pepper.

5. Place the chicken breast-side up in a roasting pan or a 9" × 13" pan and place on a rack. If you don't have a roasting rack, try using the little rack that came with your toaster oven . . . works like a charm.

6. Bake for about 1 hour 15 minutes, or until the internal temperature is 160°F. Remove the chicken from the oven, and let it rest in the pan for at least 15 minutes before cutting it.

QUICKIES

- *If you buy a chicken that has one of those little pop-up thermometers, beware: You'll surely overcook it since the thermometer pops up at 180°F instead of 160°F. Other ways to check for doneness besides using a thermometer are to see if the juices run clear and if the leg and thigh joints are loose when you pull on them.*

- *Leftovers can be used in endless ways: Seared Chicken Breast with Almond-Olive Relish (page 120), Chicken Enchiladas (page 118), Coconut Curry Chicken (116), or added to any salad for a light meal.*

carving your chicken

Legs and Thighs

Using a chef's knife, slice the skin between the leg and the body of the bird. Carefully pull the leg and thigh downward until they are about parallel with the cutting board, until the thigh joint pops. Where it pops is where you will slice the thigh away from the body. Now you're left with the leg and thigh, still attached to each other. If you want to separate them, look underneath for where the joints meet, then cut through at that point.

Breasts

Using a chef's knife, slice along the side of the breast bone that runs down the center of the body. Then, using short strokes with your knife, follow the contour of the body to loosen the breast until you can cut the entire breast off. Repeat on the other side for the remaining breast.

Wings

Pull the wings gently backward (toward the underside of the chicken) until the joint pops. Then, using a chef's knife, slice right through the joint to remove it.

Baked Chicken Smothered in Tomato Sauce and Ricotta

NUTRIENTS
Antioxidants
Calcium
Fiber
Folate

TOMATO SAUCE:

½ tablespoon extra-virgin olive oil

½ small onion, diced

2 cloves garlic, minced (or use a garlic press)

¼ bunch roughly chopped fresh basil (leaves only, no stems)

1 (14-ounce) can crushed tomatoes

Salt and pepper to taste

COOKING ACCESSORIES

Chef's knife

Garlic press (optional)

1-quart pot with lid

Bowl

Wooden spoon or spatula

Oven-safe baking dish (any from "Pots and Pans" list, page 26)

Instant-read thermometer

1. Heat the oven to 350°F.

2. Heat a 1-quart pot over medium heat and add the olive oil.

3. When the pot and oil are hot, add the onion and, stirring occasionally with a wooden spoon or heat-resistant spatula, cook about 4 minutes, or until the onion is soft and translucent but not browned.

4. Add the garlic and cook about 1 minute.

5. Add the basil and tomatoes. Bring to a boil, then reduce the heat to low and simmer 15 minutes, stirring occasionally. Season with salt and pepper.

TO FINISH:

6. While the sauce simmers, in a small bowl combine the ricotta, salt and pepper to taste, remaining basil, and chili flakes, if using.

7. Spray an oven-safe dish with cooking spray. Season both sides of the chicken breast with salt and pepper and place into the dish.

8. Spoon the ricotta mixture evenly over chicken and pour the tomato sauce on top. Bake for 30 minutes, or until the chicken reaches an internal temperature of 160°F.

Baked Chicken (cont'd)

TO FINISH:

¼ *cup ricotta cheese*

Salt and pepper to taste

¼ *bunch roughly chopped basil (leaves only, no stems)*

¼ *teaspoon crushed red chili flakes (optional)*

Cooking spray

1 boneless, skinless chicken breast

QUICKIES

- *This is a perfect freezer item. Let the chicken cool completely after baking (transfer to a freezer-safe container if necessary) and store for an easy weeknight meal. Let thaw to room temperature or in the fridge before reheating in the oven at 350°F until tomato sauce is bubbly and chicken is heated through, about 20 minutes.*

- *This recipe makes more sauce than you'll need, so freeze any extra or save it for a quick pasta dinner another night. To use again, let thaw at room temperature or in the fridge, then reheat in a small saucepan on medium low heat.*

- *For a lower fat version, try low- or nonfat ricotta cheese.*

- *To get rid of the scent of garlic from your hands, slice a lemon in half and rub it all over. The acid in the juice helps remove the odor.*

Coconut Curry Chicken

NUTRIENTS
Antioxidants
Calcium

2 chicken tenders, cut into 1" cubes

Salt and pepper to taste

1 teaspoon extra-virgin olive oil

1 shallot, thinly sliced

1 teaspoon curry powder

⅓ cup light coconut milk

¼ cup low-sodium chicken broth

Juice of a quarter lime

1 teaspoon chopped fresh cilantro
(leaves only, no stems)

1 teaspoon chopped fresh basil
(leaves only, no stems)

COOKING ACCESSORIES

Chef's knife

7" Sauté pan

Tongs

1. Season the chicken all over with salt and pepper.

2. Heat a 7" sauté pan over medium high heat and coat it with the olive oil.

3. When the pan and oil are hot, add the seasoned chicken to the pan. Let it brown on the first side for about 3 to 4 minutes, then flip with tongs and let the other side brown for another 3 to 4 minutes.

4. Stir in the shallots and cook for 30 seconds.

5. Add the curry powder, coconut milk, and chicken broth and bring to a boil. Reduce the heat to low and simmer for 5 to 7 minutes or until the chicken is cooked through. Remove the pan from the heat.

6. Add and stir in the lime juice, cilantro, and basil and season with salt and pepper.

QUICKIES

- *This dish freezes well. Once it's cooked and cooled, just wrap it tightly in plastic wrap. To use later, let thaw at room temperature or in the fridge, then reheat, covered, in the oven at 350°F for 20 to 30 minutes, or until heated through.*

- *Coconut milk comes in 15-ounce cans, so freeze what you don't need and use it next time. Or make extra sauce and freeze that: Just sauté the shallots in a little olive oil, then add curry powder, coconut milk, lime juice, cilantro, and basil. If you can't find chicken tenders, use breasts and cut them into 1" cubes.*

- *To chop herbs, gather them up into a bundle together and chop with a chef's knife.*

Simple Chicken Cutlets with Shallots and White Wine

1. Heat a 10" skillet on high and coat it with the olive oil.

2. Season the chicken with salt and pepper on both sides. When the pan and oil are hot, gently lay the chicken in the pan.

3. Cook the chicken for about 2 to 3 minutes per side, then remove it from the pan and cover to keep warm.

4. Reduce the heat to medium low. Stir in the shallots and cook until translucent.

5. Add the wine and broth and reduce the liquid by half of the original amount. Then season with salt and pepper.

6. Return the chicken to the pan and coat it with the sauce.

7. Sprinkle with chopped parsley.

QUICKIES

- *Most stores sell cutlets, but if you can't find them, simply buy a boneless/skinless breast, lay it in between two sheets of plastic wrap, and pound it with a mallet until it's ¼" thick. Don't have a mallet? Use a rolling pin or the side of a wine bottle.*

- *The flavor of wine concentrates when it cooks, so choose a wine that you won't pay an arm and a leg for. Generally you'll want a dry wine that won't impart too much sweetness into the dish. Don't waste your time with "cooking wine." It has poor flavor and is full of salt.*

- *Shallots are similar to onions but are sweeter, more delicate, and smaller—perfect for meals-for-one.*

NUTRIENTS
Antioxidants

½ tablespoon extra-virgin olive oil

2 chicken breast cutlets

Salt and pepper to taste

2 shallots, sliced

2 tablespoons white wine

½ cup chicken broth

½ tablespoon chopped fresh Italian flat-leaf parsley

COOKING ACCESSORIES
Chef's knife
10" Skillet
Tongs

Chicken Enchiladas

½ tablespoon extra-virgin olive oil

Salt and pepper to taste

1 boneless, skinless chicken breast

½ small onion, sliced

1 clove garlic, minced

½ teaspoon chipotle chili powder

½ teaspoon chili powder

½ teaspoon dried oregano

1 teaspoon ground cumin

1 (16-ounce) can crushed tomatoes

½ cup shredded Monterey jack or pepper jack cheese

2 corn or whole-wheat tortillas

2 teaspoons chopped fresh cilantro (leaves only, no stems)

COOKING ACCESSORIES

7" Sauté pan, oven-safe

Tongs

Chef's knife

Garlic press (optional)

(cont'd on facing page)

1. Heat the oven to 350°F.

2. Heat an oven-safe 7" sauté pan over medium high heat and coat it with the olive oil.

3. Season the chicken on both sides. When the pan and oil are hot, place the chicken in the pan. Let it sear for 3 to 4 minutes, or until the chicken has a nice golden crust.

4. Flip the chicken using tongs and transfer the pan to the oven and bake about 5 minutes, or until it reaches an internal temperature of 160.

5. Let the chicken cool, then shred it into small pieces and set aside in a bowl.

6. Heat a 1-quart pot over medium heat and coat it with the olive oil.

7. Add the onion, chili powder, oregano, and cumin and stir together using a wooden spoon or heat-resistant spatula. Cook for 5 to 8 minutes, until the onions are translucent.

8. Add the tomatoes and bring to a boil.

9. Turn down the heat and let it simmer for 15 minutes, stirring occasionally.

10. Combine half of the sauce and half of the cheese with the shredded chicken.

11. Fill one tortilla with half of the chicken mixture, roll it up, and place it in a small baking dish or loaf pan. Repeat with the other tortilla.

12. Cover the tortillas with the remaining sauce and cheese.

13. Bake until heated through, about 15 to 20 minutes.

14. Remove the enchiladas from the oven and sprinkle them with chopped cilantro.

QUICKIES

- *This dish freezes well once it's cooked and cooled. Just wrap it tightly in plastic wrap. To use later, thaw at room temperature or in the fridge, then reheat in a 350°F oven for 30 to 40 minutes, or until heated through.*

- *Chipotle chilies are smoked jalapeños. If you can't find chipotle powder, you can usually find canned chipotles in adobo in the Mexican foods aisle of your grocery store. You'll just want to puree that in a blender or food processor and freeze whatever you don't use. For this recipe, substitute ½ teaspoon to 1 teaspoon of chipotles in adobo, depending on how spicy you like it.*

- *Cilantro looks similar to Italian parsley, and as luck would have it they're usually next to each other in the supermarket.*

COOKING ACCESSORIES

Wooden spoon or heat-resistant spatula

Bowl

Grater

1-quart pot

9" × 5" Loaf pan or small baking dish

Seared Chicken Breast with Almond-Olive Relish

NUTRIENTS
Antioxidants

½ tablespoon extra-virgin olive oil

1 boneless, skinless chicken breast

Salt and pepper to taste

1 shallot, thinly sliced

1 tablespoon picholine (or other green) olives, chopped

1 tablespoon roasted red bell pepper, chopped

1 tablespoon coarsely chopped toasted almonds

1 teaspoon chopped fresh Italian flat-leaf parsley

COOKING ACCESSORIES

Chef's knife

7" Sauté pan or nonstick baking sheet

7" Sauté pan, oven-safe

Tongs

Wooden spoon or heat-resistant spatula

Bowl

1. Heat the oven to 350°F.

2. Heat an oven-safe 7" saute pan over medium high heat and coat it with the olive oil.

3. Season the chicken with salt and pepper on both sides.

4. Once the pan and oil are hot, place the chicken skin side down into the pan. (On a skinless breast, the "skin side" is the side where the skin once was, the smoother of the two sides.) Let it sear 4 to 5 minutes, or until the chicken has a nice brown crust.

5. Flip the chicken using tongs and transfer the pan to the oven and cook until the chicken reaches an internal temperature of 160°F, about 10 minutes.

6. Remove the chicken from the pan and return the pan to the stove over medium heat.

7. Add the shallot and cook until translucent, stirring with a wooden spoon or heat-resistant spatula.

8. In a separate bowl, add the olives, peppers, almonds, and parsley. Stir, then spoon the relish over the chicken.

QUICKIES

- *Cooking shallots and onions until translucent means until they become see-through. If the pan is too hot they will caramelize instead, so turn the heat down if necessary. Caramelizing imparts a much different flavor.*

- *Toast nuts on a baking sheet in a 300°F oven for just a few minutes. They are done cooking as soon as you can smell them. You can also toast them in a dry pan (without oil) on the stove; toss them occasionally.*

- *We recommend buying roasted red peppers in a jar rather than taking the time to roast your own.*

Pork Chops with Figs and Honey

1. Heat the oven to 350°F.

2. Heat an oven-safe 7" sauté pan over medium high heat and coat it with the olive oil.

3. Once the pan and oil are hot, season the pork chop on both sides with salt and pepper and place in the pan.

4. Let the pork chop sear for about 3 minutes, or until there is a golden crust, then flip it with tongs.

5. Transfer the pan to the oven and let the pork chop cook for about 5 to 7 minutes, or until the pork chop reaches an internal temperature of 145°F.

6. Remove the pork chop from the pan and cover it to keep it warm.

7. Place the same pan over medium high heat, wiping out any excess grease.

8. Add the figs, thyme, honey, and chicken broth.

9. Bring to a boil and let the liquids reduce by half, then season with salt and pepper if necessary.

10. Spoon the fig mixture over the pork chop.

QUICKIE

● *The most common type of fig is the Black Mission Fig. It has a deep purple skin and is oval in shape. Dried figs are a delicious snack and are packed full of iron and calcium.*

NUTRIENTS
Antioxidants
Calcium

½ tablespoon extra-virgin olive oil

1 bone-in pork chop, any excess fat trimmed

Salt and pepper to taste

2 tablespoons diced dried figs, about 2 whole figs

1 teaspoon chopped fresh thyme (leaves only, no stems)

1 teaspoon honey

1 teaspoon balsamic vinegar

⅓ cup low-sodium chicken broth

COOKING ACCESSORIES
Chef's knife
7" Sauté pan, oven-safe
Tongs
Instant-read thermometer

Pork Chops with Parsley, Mint, Lemon, and Chili Flakes

1 teaspoon extra-virgin olive oil

1 bone-in pork chop, any excess fat trimmed

Salt and pepper to taste

1 tablespoon white wine

⅓ cup low-sodium chicken broth

Juice of half a lemon

1 clove garlic, crushed with the side of a knife

1 tablespoon chopped fresh Italian flat-leaf parsley

1 teaspoon chopped fresh mint

Zest of half a lemon

¼ teaspoon crushed red chili flakes, or to taste

COOKING ACCESSORIES

Chef's knife

7" Sauté pan, oven-safe

Tongs

Instant-read thermometer

1. Heat the oven to 350°F.

2. Heat an oven-safe 7" sauté pan over medium high heat and coat it with the olive oil.

3. Once the pan and oil are hot, season the chop on both sides with salt and pepper and place in the pan.

4. Let the pork chop sear for about 3 minutes, or until there is a golden crust, then flip it with tongs.

5. Transfer the pan to the oven and cook for about 5 to 7 minutes, or until the chop reaches an internal temperature of 145°F.

6. Remove the pork chop and cover it to keep it warm. Return the pan to the stove over medium high heat, wiping out any excess grease.

7. Add the wine, broth, lemon juice, and garlic and let it reduce by half. Stir in the parsley, mint, lemon zest, and chili flakes. Remove the clove of garlic, and spoon over the chop.

QUICKIES

- *The easiest way to zest a lemon is to use a microplane. Just be careful to remove only the yellow part of the skin because the white pith is very bitter. If you don't have a microplane, you can peel the skin off using a vegetable peeler and finely chop it with a knife.*

- *To chop herbs, gather them up into a bundle together and chop with a chef's knife.*

- *To get rid of the scent of garlic from your hands, slice a lemon in half and rub it all over. The acid in the juice helps remove the odor.*

Saltimboca-Style Pork Tenderloin with Prosciutto and Sage

This recipe serves about three, so after cooking, use just ⅓ of the tenderloin for a meal-for-one.

1. Heat the oven to 350°F.

2. Heat an oven-safe 10" sauté pan over medium high heat and add the oil.

3. Once the pan and oil are hot, season the pork tenderloin on all sides with salt and pepper and place in the pan. Let the pork sear until golden brown, about 3 to 4 minutes, flip with tongs and then transfer it to the oven.

4. Roast the pork about 13 to 15 minutes or until it reaches an internal temperature of 140°F.

5. Remove the pork and cover it to keep it warm. Return the pan to the stove over medium heat. Wipe out any excess grease.

6. Stir in the shallots and prosciutto and cook until soft but not browned, 2 to 3 minutes.

7. Add wine and reduce the liquid until it is almost entirely evaporated. Add the chicken broth and reduce the liquid by half. Then stir in the sage.

8. Slice the pork into ½" slices and place on a plate. Pour the sauce over the pork. Squeeze fresh lemon juice over the top.

QUICKIE

- *Pork tenderloins often come in packs of two, so freeze one and save it for another recipe, such as Pork Tenderloin with Romesco Sauce (page 124) or Hoisin-Glazed Pork Tenderloin (page 125).*

NUTRIENTS
Antioxidants

1 teaspoon extra-virgin olive oil
1 pork tenderloin
Salt and pepper to taste
2 shallots, sliced
2 tablespoons white wine
½ cup low-sodium chicken broth
1 teaspoon chopped fresh sage
2 slices prosciutto, sliced in ¼" strips
2 lemon wedges

COOKING ACCESSORIES
Chef's knife
10" Sauté pan, oven-safe
Tongs
Instant-read thermometer

Pork Tenderloin with Romesco Sauce

NUTRIENTS
Antioxidants
Calcium
Fiber
Folate

1 clove garlic, peeled and chopped

1 roasted red bell pepper

¼ cup toasted almonds

Juice of half a lemon

1 tablespoon extra-virgin olive oil

Salt and pepper to taste

½ tablespoon extra-virgin olive oil

1 pork tenderloin

COOKING ACCESSORIES

Chef's knife

Food processor

10" Skillet, oven-safe

Tongs

This recipe serves about three, so after cooking, use just ⅓ of the tenderloin for a meal-for-one.

1. Heat the oven to 350°F.

2. In a food processor, combine the garlic, bell pepper, almonds, lemon juice, 1 tablespoon olive oil, salt, and pepper until well blended and smooth.

3. Heat an oven-safe 10" sauté pan over medium heat and add ½ tablespoon of the olive oil.

4. Season the pork tenderloin on all sides with salt and pepper and place it in the hot pan. Let it sear until golden brown, about 3 to 4 minutes.

5. Flip the pork using tongs and transfer the pan to the oven and bake for about 13 to 15 minutes, or until the internal temperature reaches 140°F.

6. Remove the pan from the oven and let the pork sit for 5 to 10 minutes. Then slice it into ½" slices and spoon the sauce over them.

QUICKIES

- *Romesco sauce is a traditional Spanish sauce that can also be served with fish or chicken.*

- *You can freeze any leftover Romesco Sauce. Just store in a freezer-safe container, placing plastic wrap directly on the surface to prevent freezer burn. To use again, thaw at room temperature or in the fridge.*

- *Toast nuts on a baking sheet in a 300°F oven for just a few minutes. They are done cooking as soon as you can smell them. Overcooking them will burn their oils and they'll become bitter. You can also toast them in a dry pan (without oil) on the stove; toss them occasionally.*

Hoisin-Glazed Pork Tenderloin

This recipe serves about three, so after cooking, use just ⅓ of the tenderloin for a meal-for-one.

1. Heat the oven to 350°F.

2. Combine the Hoisin sauce, garlic, ginger, and soy sauce in a bowl.

3. Heat an oven-safe 10" sauté pan over high heat and coat it with the olive oil.

4. Once the pan and oil are hot, season the pork on all sides with the salt and pepper and place it in the pan. Let it sear for about 3 minutes, or until there is a nice brown crust.

5. Flip the pork over and brush liberally with the Hoisin mixture.

6. Transfer the pan to the oven and bake for about 13 to 15 minutes or until the pork reaches an internal temperature of 145°F. Let the pork sit for 5 to 10 minutes.

7. Slice the pork into ½" slices and spoon any extra Hoisin mixture over them.

8. Sprinkle with scallions.

QUICKIES

- *Hoisin is a sweet, thick sauce made from soybeans, garlic and spices. It can be found on the Asian foods aisle of your grocery store.*

- *Extra Hoisin Glaze can be frozen. Just store in a freezer-safe container and place plastic wrap directly on the glaze to prevent freezer burn. To use later, thaw at room temperature or in the fridge.*

- *To peel ginger, see page 79.*

NUTRIENTS
Antioxidants

¼ cup Hoisin sauce

2 cloves garlic, chopped (or use a garlic press)

1" piece of fresh ginger, peeled and minced (or grated with a microplane)

2 tablespoons low-sodium soy sauce

½ tablespoon extra-virgin olive oil

1 pork tenderloin

Salt and pepper to taste

2 tablespoons scallions, sliced thin

COOKING ACCESSORIES
Chef's knife

Garlic press (optional)

Microplane (optional)

Bowl

10" Skillet, oven-safe

Tongs

Grilled Flank Steak with Latin American Chimichurri Sauce

1 clove garlic, chopped

¼ bunch (about 1 small handful) fresh Italian flat-leaf parsley, tough stems removed

¼ bunch (1 small handful) fresh cilantro, tough stems removed

Juice of half a lime

1 teaspoon red wine vinegar

1½ tablespoons extra-virgin olive oil

½ jalapeño, seeded (optional)

Salt and pepper to taste

Extra-virgin olive oil to brush on the grill, about 1 teaspoon

1 (4- to 6-ounce) piece of flank steak, excess fat trimmed

COOKING ACCESSORIES

Chef's knife

Garlic press (optional)

Food processor

Grill pan

Tongs

1. To make the chimichurri sauce, combine the garlic, parsley, cilantro, lime juice, vinegar, 1½ tablespoons olive oil, and jalapeño in a food processor. Blend until sauce is well combined but still slightly chunky. Season with salt and pepper.

2. Heat a grill or grill pan on high heat.

3. Once the grill is hot, use a paper towel to rub the grill with the remaining 1 teaspoon olive oil to prevent the meat from sticking.

4. Coat the flank steak with half of the chimichurri sauce and salt and pepper on both sides to taste.

5. Place on the hot grill. Let it sit, undisturbed, for about 4 minutes. Then flip it with tongs and continue cooking for about 3 to 5 minutes, depending on the desired doneness (see page 110).

6. Remove the meat from the grill and let it sit for 5 to 10 minutes, then slice into ½" pieces. Be sure to cut the meat *against* the grain or it will be tough. To do this, look at the meat and you will see the fibers of the meat running in one direction. Simply make your slices perpendicular to these fibers. Pour the remaining chimichurri over the meat.

QUICKIES

- *If you don't have a grill, a great option is a grill pan that can be used on your stovetop. You can find these at any kitchen store or, for a bargain, go to a restaurant supply store like Smart & Final.*

- *Extra chimichurri sauce can be frozen. Just store in a freezer-safe container and place plastic wrap directly on the sauce to prevent freezer burn. To use later, thaw at room temperature or in the fridge.*

Grilled Flank Steak with Sweet Chili and Soy

1. In a small bowl, combine the chili garlic sauce, honey, lime juice, soy sauce, garlic, scallion, salt, and pepper.

2. Heat a grill or grill pan on medium high heat. Once the grill is hot, use a paper towel to rub the remaining 1 teaspoon olive oil on the grill to prevent the meat from sticking.

3. Coat the meat with half of the sweet chili mixture and salt and pepper to taste on both sides. Place the meat on the hot grill. Let it sit, undisturbed, about 4 minutes, then flip it with tongs and continue cooking for about 3 to 5 minutes or until the desired doneness (see page 110).

4. Remove the meat from the grill and let it sit for 5 to 10 minutes, then slice it into ½" slices. Be sure to cut the meat *against* the grain or it will be tough. To do this, look at the meat and you will see the fibers of the meat running in one direction. Simply make your slices perpendicular to these fibers. Pour the remaining sauce over the meat.

QUICKIES

● *Flank steak stands up very well to marinating. A great timesaver is to marinate the meat in the refrigerator the night before, and you'll have a super-quick, flavorful dinner when you get home after a long day.*

● *Leftover Sweet Chili and Soy mixture can be frozen. Just store in a freezer-safe container and place plastic wrap directly on the mixture to prevent freezer burn. To use later, thaw at room temperature or in the fridge.*

● *Chili garlic sauce can be found in the Asian section of your local market.*

NUTRIENTS
Antioxidants

½ tablespoon chili garlic sauce

1 tablespoon honey

Juice of half a lime

1 tablespoon light soy sauce

1 clove garlic, minced (or use a garlic press)

1 tablespoon chopped scallion or green onion (about ¼ a scallion)

Salt and pepper to taste

1 teaspoon extra-virgin olive oil to brush on the grill

1 (4- to 6-ounce) piece flank steak, excess fat trimmed

COOKING ACCESSORIES
Bowl

Chef's knife

Garlic press (optional)

Grill pan

Tongs

Beef Filet Mignon with Mustard and Herb Crust

NUTRIENTS
Antioxidants

1 tablespoon whole-grain or Dijon mustard

1 clove garlic, minced (or use a garlic press)

1 teaspoon chopped fresh thyme (leaves only, no stems)

1 teaspoon chopped fresh Italian flat-leaf parsley

1 teaspoon chopped fresh rosemary (leaves only, no stems)

Salt and pepper to taste

½ tablespoon extra-virgin olive oil

1 (4- to 6-ounce) filet mignon

COOKING ACCESSORIES

Bowl

Chef's knife

Garlic press (optional)

Baking sheet or small oven-safe baking dish

1. Heat oven to 400°F.

2. Combine the mustard, garlic, and herbs in a bowl. Season both sides of the beef liberally with salt and pepper, then coat it with the mustard mixture.

3. Place the filet on a baking sheet or small oven-safe baking dish. Roast the meat for 12 to 15 minutes, or until desired doneness (see page 110).

QUICKIES

- *This type of herb crust is very versatile. Try using it on chicken, pork, or hearty fish like salmon and tuna.*

- *To chop herbs, gather them up into a bundle together and chop with a chef's knife.*

Classic American Burger

1. Combine the salt, pepper, Worcestershire sauce, steak sauce, garlic powder, and beef in a bowl. Combine well, but do not overmix or the meat will become too tough.

2. Form into a patty that is about the same size as the bun you're using.

3. To grill, place the burger over medium high heat on an oiled hot grill or grill pan for about 2 to 3 minutes per side, flipping with tongs or a spatula, until the desired doneness (see page 110). To pan-sear, heat a skillet over medium high heat and coat it with the olive oil. Place the burger in the hot skillet and let it cook for about 2 to 3 minutes per side until the desired doneness. If you're using cheese, add it about a minute before the meat is done cooking so it has time to melt.

4. Toast the bun in the toaster, or directly on the grill, while the meat is cooking.

5. Top the toasted bun with the burger and pile high with arugula, tomatoes, and condiments of your choice!

QUICKIES

- *To get some extra calcium, make it a cheeseburger. For extra fiber and whole grains, use a whole-grain bun.*

- *Get creative. Spice up your ordinary burgers with Basil Pesto (page 231), Sun-Dried Tomato Pesto (page 235), Romesco Sauce (page 235), olive tapenade, or avocado. Top one with Mushroom Ragout (page 81) and Caramelized Onions (page 84). Try tossing the arugula in your favorite vinaigrette before building your burger.*

NUTRIENTS

Antioxidants Folate
Calcium* Whole Grain
Fiber

*contains calcium only if made with cheese

½ teaspoon salt

½ teaspoon pepper

1 teaspoon Worcestershire sauce

1 teaspoon steak sauce

¼ teaspoon garlic powder

¼ pound 90% lean ground beef

½ teaspoon extra-virgin olive oil for coating the grill

1 slice Swiss cheese (optional) or cheese of your choice

1 whole-wheat bun, or fresh-baked bun from your local grocery store

¼ cup arugula

2 slices tomato

Condiments of choice

COOKING ACCESSORIES

Bowl

Grill pan or 7" sauté pan

Tongs or spatula

Serrated knife to slice tomatoes

Curried Scallops

Antioxidants
Omega-3

½ tablespoon extra-virgin olive oil

4 large sea scallops

Salt and pepper

1 teaspoon curry powder

Lime juice to taste

1. Heat the 7" sauté pan over medium high heat and coat it with the olive oil.

2. Season both sides of each scallop with salt and pepper, and coat evenly with curry powder. Carefully add the scallops to the hot skillet and cook about 2½ minutes per side, turning them with tongs and being careful not to overcook.

3. Squeeze a little fresh lime juice over each scallop.

QUICKIES

- *Depending on your taste, scallops are actually delicious when they are cooked medium rare (as prepared in this recipe), so give it a try.*

- *When buying scallops, look for ones that are plump and moist with no discoloration. Sometimes they have a small muscle still attached to the side, which can be easily cut off.*

COOKING ACCESSORIES

7" Sauté pan

Tongs

Scallops with Melted Leeks and Thyme

1. Heat a 7" sauté pan over low heat and coat with ½ tablespoon olive oil.

2. When the pan and oil are heated, add the leeks, salt, and pepper. Cook until the leeks are very soft, about 10 minutes. Stir occasionally with a wooden spoon or heat-resistant spatula.

3. Add the wine and broth and let the liquids reduce (boil down) by half, then stir in the thyme. Transfer the leek mixture to a small bowl and cover it to keep it warm.

4. Return the skillet to medium high heat and coat it with ½ tablespoon olive oil. Season both sides of each scallop with salt and pepper and place them in the hot skillet.

5. Cook about 2 minutes per side, flipping them with tongs, being careful not to overcook them. Spoon the leek mixture over each scallop.

QUICKIES

● *Depending on your taste, scallops are actually delicious when they are cooked medium rare (as prepared in this recipe), so give it a try.*

● *Leeks look like giant green onions/scallions. They're found in the refrigerated produce section, usually near cabbages and Swiss chard. They're often dirty, since they grow in the ground, so the best way to clean them is to first cut them according to the recipe (¼" half moons, for example), then fill a bowl with cold water and drop the leeks in. Swish them around with your hand, and all of the dirt will fall to the bottom of the bowl; then scoop them up with your hands or a slotted spoon.*

NUTRIENTS
Antioxidants
Calcium
Folate
Omega-3

½ tablespoon extra-virgin olive oil

½ small leek, cut in half lengthwise, then crosswise into ¼" half moons

Salt and pepper to taste

1 tablespoon white wine

⅓ cup low-sodium chicken broth

1½ teaspoons chopped fresh thyme (leaves only, no stems)

4 large sea scallops

COOKING ACCESSORIES
Chef's knife

7" Sauté pan

Small bowl

Wooden spoon or heat-resistant spatula

Tongs

Fish Tacos with Avocado and Lime

NUTRIENTS

Antioxidants   Folate
Calcium   Omega-3
Fiber   Whole Grain

Juice of half a lime

¼ teaspoon ground cumin

Pinch of dried oregano

¼ cup pre-shredded cabbage, red or green

1 teaspoon scallion, thinly sliced

Salt and pepper to taste

½ tablespoon extra-virgin olive oil

1 (4- to 6-ounce) halibut fillet

1 whole-wheat tortilla

2 slices avocado, seasoned with salt and pepper to taste

1 tablespoon fire-roasted salsa

COOKING ACCESSORIES

Bowl

Chef's knife

7" Sauté pan

Tongs

1. Combine the lime juice, cumin, oregano, cabbage, scallion, and salt and pepper in a bowl. Set aside.

2. Heat a 7" sauté pan over medium high heat and coat it with the olive oil.

3. Season both sides of the halibut with salt and pepper and place in the hot skillet. Cook for about 3 to 4 minutes per side, flipping it with tongs.

4. Meanwhile, heat the tortilla directly on a low-heat burner or in a toaster oven.

5. Slightly break up the halibut with the tongs, then fill the tortilla with the halibut, cabbage mixture, avocado, and salsa.

QUICKIES

- *If you can't find halibut, red snapper is a great substitute.*

- *Peeling and seeding an avocado is easy! Insert a knife at the top of the avocado and cut down until it reaches the seed, then run the knife around the entire avocado. Twist the two halves in opposite directions until they separate. To remove the seed, carefully hit the seed with the blade of the knife, so that the blade sticks in the seed. Then, holding the half in your other hand, twist it until the seed pops out. Carefully pull the seed off the knife with a dish towel. Now you're left with two seedless halves. To peel them, run a spoon right between the skin and the flesh of the avocado.*

- *Keep your cut avocados green by squeezing a little lemon juice on them before wrapping in plastic wrap or putting in an airtight container.*

Miso-Marinated Halibut

1. In a small bowl, whisk together the miso, mirin, honey, soy sauce, garlic, and ginger. Transfer this mixture to a zip-top plastic bag, add the halibut, and marinate in the refrigerator for at least 2 hours, and up to 6. (This is one of the rare instances where marinating fish longer than 15 minutes is okay.)

2. Heat the oven to 500°F.

3. Spray a baking sheet lightly with cooking spray.

4. Remove the fish from the marinade and drain off any excess. Season it lightly on both sides with salt and pepper and place it on the baking sheet. Broil it for 5 to 7 minutes, depending on the thickness of the fish. It should be flaky and slightly firm but not dry. Remove the fish from the baking sheet with a spatula.

QUICKIES

- *If you can't find halibut, try red snapper, mahi-mahi, or tilapia.*

- *Miso, a flavor staple in Japan, is simply fermented soybean paste. It can be found in either the Asian foods aisle or the specialty refrigerated section of your grocery store.*

- *Mirin is a sweet Japanese cooking wine also found in, surprise, the Asian food section of the grocery store.*

- *Extra Miso Marinade can be frozen. Just store in a freezer-safe container and place plastic wrap directly on the marinade to prevent freezer burn. To use later, thaw at room temperature or in the fridge.*

NUTRIENTS
Antioxidants
Calcium
Omega-3

1 tablespoon sweet white miso paste

2 tablespoons mirin wine

½ tablespoon honey

1 teaspoon light soy sauce

1 small clove garlic, minced (or use a garlic press)

½ teaspoon fresh ginger, peeled and minced (or grated with a microplane)

1 (4- to 6-ounce) halibut fillet

Cooking spray

Salt and pepper to taste

COOKING ACCESSORIES
Small bowl
Whisk
Garlic press (optional)
Microplane (optional)
Nonstick baking sheet
Spatula

Pistachio and Citrus Crusted Halibut

NUTRIENTS
Antioxidants
Calcium
Omega-3

2 tablespoons toasted and finely chopped pistachios (chop with a chef's knife or food processor)

Zest of one lemon

1 small clove garlic, minced (or use a garlic press)

1 teaspoon extra-virgin olive oil

1 (4- to 6-ounce) halibut fillet

Salt and pepper to taste

COOKING ACCESSORIES
Chef's knife
Microplane
Garlic press (optional)
Brush
Nonstick baking sheet
Spatula

1. Heat the oven to 400°F.

2. Combine the pistachios, lemon zest, and garlic on a small plate.

3. Brush the olive oil on the halibut and season both sides with salt and pepper.

4. Roll the fish in the pistachio mixture, carefully pressing the mixture into the fish so that it sticks.

5. Place the fish on a baking sheet and bake for 15 to 18 minutes. Remove it with a spatula.

QUICKIES

- *If you can't find halibut, look for red snapper, mahi-mahi, swordfish, or salmon.*

- *A cooking trick that decreases your cleanup time is to place aluminum foil on the baking sheet. When you're finished cooking the fish, simply lift off and discard the foil. Poof!*

- *Toast nuts on a baking sheet in a 300°F oven for just a few minutes. They are done cooking as soon as you can smell them. Overcooking them will burn their oils and they'll become bitter. You can also toast them in a dry pan (without oil) on the stove; toss them occasionally.*

- *The easiest way to zest a lemon is to use a microplane. Just be careful to remove only the yellow part of the skin because the white pith is very bitter. If you don't have a microplane, you can peel the skin off using a vegetable peeler and finely chop it with a knife.*

Maple-Dijon Salmon

1. Heat the oven to 350°F.

2. In a small bowl, combine the mustard, syrup, and scallions.

3. Coat the salmon in the olive oil and season both sides with salt and pepper.

4. Place the fillet, skin side down, on a baking sheet and brush with half the mustard mixture.

5. Bake the fillet for about 7 minutes, then brush it with the remaining mustard mixture.

6. Bake the fillet for another 5 to 7 minutes, or until the desired doneness. Remove the salmon from the baking sheet with a spatula.

QUICKIES

- *Salmon is great when cooked medium rare so that the middle is still pink and very tender . . . it melts in your mouth!*

- *If you get home from the store and realize that there are still bones in your salmon, the best way to easily remove them is with a pair of (clean) needle-nose pliers.*

- *A cooking trick that decreases your cleanup time is to place aluminum foil on the baking sheet. When you're finished cooking the fish, simply lift off and discard the foil. Poof!*

NUTRIENTS
Antioxidants
Omega-3

½ tablespoon Dijon mustard

½ tablespoon maple syrup (use sugar-free for fewer calories)

1 teaspoon finely chopped scallion or green onion. Use both the white and green parts, but remember to trim off the root.

1 (4- to 6-ounce) salmon fillet (make sure all bones are removed)

2 teaspoons extra-virgin olive oil

Salt and pepper to taste

COOKING ACCESSORIES
Bowl
Chef's knife
Nonstick baking sheet
Brush
Spatula

Ginger-Soy Marinated Tuna

NUTRIENTS
Antioxidants
Omega-3

2 tablespoons light soy sauce

1 teaspoon fresh ginger, peeled and minced (or grated with a microplane)

Juice of half a lime

1 small clove garlic, minced (or use a garlic press)

1 scallion or green onion, finely chopped. Use both the green and white parts, but remember to trim off the root.

1 (4- to 6-ounce) tuna steak

1 teaspoon extra-virgin olive oil for brushing on the grill

Salt and pepper to taste

COOKING ACCESSORIES
Bowl

Microplane (optional)

Garlic press (optional)

Chef's knife

Grill pan

Tongs

1. In a bowl, combine the soy sauce, ginger, lime, garlic, and scallion.

2. Place the tuna in a zip-top bag with half of the ginger-soy marinade and squeeze out excess air so that the tuna is completely covered in the marinade. Let it sit for 15 minutes.

3. Heat a grill or grill pan on high heat. Using a paper towel, rub olive oil onto the heated grill to prevent the tuna from sticking.

4. Remove the tuna from the marinade. Allow excess to drip off or it will burn. Season both sides of the tuna to taste with salt and pepper.

5. Place the tuna carefully on the hot grill and cook about 1½ to 2 minutes per side, leaving the tuna rare in the middle. Remove the tuna to a plate. For a more dramatic presentation, slice the tuna and fan it out on the plate.

6. Spoon the extra marinade over the tuna.

QUICKIES

- *Fish should only be marinated about 15 minutes or else it begins to break down and the texture becomes undesirable.*

- *Extra Ginger-Soy Marinade can be frozen. Just store in a freezer-safe container and place plastic wrap directly on marinade to prevent freezer burn. To use later, thaw at room temperature or in the fridge.*

Seared Pepperonata Tuna Steak

1. Heat the 7" sauté pan over medium low heat and coat it with ½ tablespoon olive oil.

2. When the pan and oil are heated, add the bell peppers and cook them until very soft (but not browned), about 15 minutes. Add the vinegar and cook another 1 minute. Add the garlic and cook it until fragrant, about 10 seconds.

3. Stir in the olives, capers, salt, pepper, and basil and remove the pan from the heat. Cover to keep warm.

4. Heat a separate skillet over high heat and coat it with ½ tablespoon olive oil.

5. Season the tuna on both sides with salt and pepper and place it carefully in the hot skillet.

6. Cook the tuna about 1½ to 2 minutes per side, leaving the tuna rare in the middle.

7. Remove the tuna to a plate, and spoon the pepperonata mixture over the tuna.

QUICKIES

- *Capers are sold either brined or salted. If brined, just drain them; if salted, rinse in cold water and drain.*

- *Extra Pepperonata can be frozen. Just store in a freezer-safe container and place plastic wrap directly on the pepperonata to prevent freezer burn. To use later, thaw at room temperature or in the fridge.*

NUTRIENTS
Antioxidants
Fiber
Folate
Omega-3

½ tablespoon extra-virgin olive oil

½ small red bell pepper, seeded and cut into ⅛" strips

1 teaspoon balsamic vinegar

1 clove garlic, minced (or use a garlic press)

½ tablespoon pitted and chopped black kalamata olives

½ tablespoon capers, drained

Salt and pepper to taste

1 teaspoon chopped fresh basil (leaves only, no stems)

½ tablespoon extra-virgin olive oil

1 (4- to 6-ounce) tuna steak

COOKING ACCESSORIES
Chef's knife

Garlic press (optional)

7" Sauté pans (for both steps 1 and 4)

Tongs

Scampi-Style Shrimp

NUTRIENTS
Antioxidants
Omega-3

½ tablespoon extra-virgin olive oil

1 clove garlic, chopped (or use a garlic press)

1 tablespoon white wine or sherry

¼ pound medium-sized shrimp, peeled and de-veined

Salt and pepper to taste

½ tablespoon chopped fresh Italian flat-leaf parsley

¼ teaspoon crushed red chili flakes (optional)

COOKING ACCESSORIES

Chef's knife

Garlic press (optional)

7" Sauté pan

Tongs

1. Heat a 7" sauté pan over medium heat and coat it with the olive oil.

2. When the pan and oil are heated, stir in the garlic and cook until fragrant, about 10 seconds.

3. Add the wine and let it reduce (boil down) by half.

4. Season the shrimp with salt and pepper on both sides and add to the pan. Cook for about 1 minute per side, flipping with tongs, or until just pink. Do not overcook or the shrimp will become rubbery.

5. Stir in the parsley, and the chili flakes if desired.

QUICKIE

- *You can buy shrimp that have already been peeled and de-veined. To do it yourself, twist off the tail and peel the shell off, making sure to remove all of the legs. To de-vein, run a paring knife along the back of the shrimp (the opposite side from where the legs were) just deep enough to expose the vein. The vein can range from a dark color to translucent. Pull it out with the tip of the knife.*

Garlicky Steamed Mussels

1. Heat a 7" sauté pan over medium heat and coat it with the olive oil.

2. When the pan and oil are heated, add the garlic and red pepper flakes and cook about 1 minute. Take care not to brown the garlic or it will become bitter.

3. Add the wine, lemon juice, clam juice or broth, and mussels.

4. Cover with a lid and cook 2 to 3 minutes, or until all of the mussels have opened, discarding any that have not.

5. Sprinkle with chopped parsley.

QUICKIES

- *If, when cleaning mussels, you come across an open one, give it a squeeze. If it closes up, it's good; if not, discard it.*
- *Italian flat-leaf parsley has much better flavor than curly parsley. It's usually next to curly parsley in the grocery store and, yes, it has flat leaves, which are pretty easy to distinguish.*
- *To get rid of the scent of garlic from your hands, slice a lemon in half and rub it all over. The acid in the juice helps remove the odor.*

NUTRIENTS
Antioxidants
Omega-3

½ tablespoon extra-virgin olive oil

1 clove garlic, thinly sliced (or use a garlic press)

¼ teaspoon crushed red pepper flakes

2 tablespoons dry white wine, such as Pinot Grigio

Juice of half a lemon

¼ cup clam juice or vegetable broth

¼ pound mussels, scrubbed and rinsed very well

2 teaspoons chopped fresh Italian flat-leaf parsley

COOKING ACCESSORIES
Chef's knife
Garlic press (optional)
7" Sauté pan with lid
Tongs

Mushroom Ragout and Spinach Frittata with Goat Cheese

NUTRIENTS
Antioxidants
Calcium
Folate

½ tablespoon butter or extra-virgin olive oil

1½ cups assorted fresh mushrooms (button, portobello, shiitake), cleaned and sliced into ¼" pieces

1 small shallot, chopped

Salt and pepper to taste

1 small clove garlic, minced

1 tablespoon white wine (or sherry)

1 large handful fresh spinach, rinsed

½ teaspoon chopped fresh thyme (leaves only, no stems)

Cooking spray

8 egg whites or 4 whole eggs (should be about 1 cup)

1 ounce goat cheese, crumbled

COOKING ACCESSORIES

Chef's knife

Garlic press (optional)

10" (or larger) skillet

Wooden spoon or heat-resistant spatula

7" Sauté pan, nonstick and oven-safe

Bowl

MAKES 2 SERVINGS

1. Heat the oven to 350°F.

2. Melt the butter or pour the olive oil in a 10" skillet over medium high heat.

3. When the pan and oil are hot, add the mushrooms, shallots, salt, and pepper and sauté for about 5 minutes, or until the mushrooms begin to soften and most of the moisture that comes out of the mushrooms evaporates.

4. Add the garlic and cook until fragrant (only 10 seconds or so).

5. Add the wine and scrape up any browned bits from the bottom of the pan. Let the wine cook down and evaporate until the pan is almost dry.

6. Stir in the spinach and cook until just wilted, about 30 seconds. Stir in the thyme.

7. Coat a separate 7" nonstick, oven-safe sauté pan with cooking spray and heat it over medium heat.

8. In a separate bowl, lightly beat the egg whites or eggs with a fork until they are slightly frothy. Stir in the cooled mushroom-spinach mixture and the goat cheese.

9. Pour the egg mixture into the heated pan and let it set for about 30 seconds. Transfer the pan to the oven and bake for about 10 minutes, or until the eggs have just set all the way through and don't jiggle. Remove the frittata from the skillet immediately.

Mushroom Ragout and Spinach Frittata (cont'd)

QUICKIES

- *Frittatas are a great way to use up leftovers. If you had this mushroom ragout as a side dish, or a topping on fish or chicken, save the rest for the next night's frittata.*

- *Goat cheese is a soft, white cheese that has a delightful tangy flavor. You can find it mixed with herbs, pepper, or even ash, or wrapped in edible leaves, to name just a few variations. You can store it in your fridge for up to 2 weeks, as long as it's tightly wrapped in plastic.*

- *The best way to remove the frittata from the pan is to place a larger-sized plate directly on top of the pan, then flip it so the frittata drops onto the plate.*

- *To chop herbs, gather them up into a bundle together and chop with a chef's knife.*

- *The flavor of wine concentrates when it cooks, so choose a wine that you won't pay an arm and a leg for. Generally you'll want a dry wine that won't impart too much sweetness into the dish. Don't waste your time with "cooking wine." It has poor flavor and is full of salt.*

Caramelized Onion Frittata *with* Parmesan *and* Balsamic Glaze

NUTRIENTS

Antioxidants

Calcium

Low-fat*

This recipe is low-fat only if made with egg whites.

1 teaspoon extra-virgin olive oil

½ onion (preferably a sweet onion like Vidalia or Maui, but any onion will do), sliced into ⅛" slices

Salt and pepper to taste

Cooking spray

8 egg whites or 4 whole eggs (should be about 1 cup)

1 ounce grated Parmesan cheese

2 tablespoons balsamic vinegar

COOKING ACCESSORIES

Chef's knife

10" Skillet for the onions

Bowl for mixing ingredients

Wooden spoon or heat-resistant spatula

7" Sauté pan, nonstick and oven-safe

1-quart pot (or smaller)

Brush

MAKES 2 SERVINGS

1. Heat the oven to 350°F.

2. Heat the oil in a 10" skillet pan over low heat. When the pan is heated, add the onions, salt, and pepper. Cook slowly until the onions are very soft and a deep brown, stirring occasionally with a wooden spoon or heat-resistant spatula.

3. Coat a 7" nonstick, oven-safe skillet with cooking spray and heat it over medium heat.

4. In a separate bowl, lightly beat the egg whites or eggs with a fork until they are slightly frothy. Stir in the caramelized onions and Parmesan.

5. Pour the egg mixture into the heated 7" sauté pan and let it set for about 30 seconds. Transfer the pan to the oven and bake for about 10 minutes, or until the eggs have just set all the way through and don't jiggle. Remove the frittata from the pan immediately.

6. Meanwhile, heat the balsamic vinegar in a 1-quart (or smaller) pot over medium heat until it reduces to a syrup. Watch it carefully because it will happen quickly.

7. Remove the frittata from the oven and turn it onto a plate. Brush the balsamic glaze over the frittata.

QUICKIE

- *The best way to remove the frittata from the pan is to place a larger-sized plate directly on top of the pan, then flip it so the frittata drops onto the plate.*

Spinach, Bacon, and Fontina Frittata

MAKES 2 SERVINGS

1. Heat the oven to 350°F.

2. Heat a 7" nonstick, oven-safe sauté pan over medium low heat. Cook the bacon until it reaches your desired level of crispness. Drain it on a paper towel. Crumble it when cool to the touch.

3. Wipe the bacon grease out of the skillet, then heat the skillet over medium heat and add the olive oil. Add the shallot and cook for about 2 minutes, or until shallot is soft and translucent but not browned. Add the spinach and cook it briefly, until it is wilted but not browned, about 30 seconds. Season spinach to taste with salt and pepper and remove it from the pan.

4. Coat the same 7" nonstick sauté pan with cooking spray and heat it over medium heat.

5. In a separate bowl, lightly beat the egg whites with a fork until they're slightly frothy. Stir in the bacon pieces, cooled spinach mixture, and fontina. Pour the egg mixture into the heated nonstick skillet and let it set for 30 seconds. Transfer the skillet to the oven and bake for 10 minutes, or until the eggs have set all the way through and don't jiggle. Remove the frittata from the pan immediately.

QUICKIES

- *The best way to remove the frittata from the pan is to place a larger-sized plate directly on top of the pan, then flip it so the frittata drops onto the plate.*

- *Make this recipe healthier by substituting turkey bacon for the bacon. We know, we know, sometimes it hurts.*

NUTRIENTS

Antioxidants

Calcium

Folate

---

1 slice bacon

1 teaspoon extra-virgin olive oil

1 small shallot, sliced

1 large handful spinach

Salt and pepper to taste

Cooking spray

8 egg whites, or 4 whole eggs (should be about 1 cup)

½ ounce fontina cheese, cut into small pieces

COOKING ACCESSORIES

Chef's knife

7" Sauté pan, nonstick and oven-safe

Bowl

Tongs

Grilled Asparagus Frittata with Tomato and Basil Salsa

4 spears asparagus, ends trimmed

½ teaspoon extra-virgin olive oil

Salt and pepper to taste

1 small tomato, diced

1 tablespoon chopped fresh basil leaves (leaves only, no stems)

½ small clove garlic, minced (or use a garlic press)

1 teaspoon good extra-virgin olive oil

Salt and pepper to taste

Cooking spray

8 egg whites or 4 whole eggs (should be about 1 cup)

COOKING ACCESSORIES

Chef's knife

Barbecue or grill pan

Garlic press (optional)

Bowl

7" Sauté pan, nonstick and oven-safe

MAKES 2 SERVINGS

1. Heat the oven to 350°F.

2. Heat the barbecue or grill pan on medium high heat.

3. Trim the ends off the asparagus, about the bottom 1½ inches. Toss the asparagus in the olive oil, salt, and pepper.

4. Place the asparagus on the hot grill and let it cook until you can see grill marks. Flip them over with tongs and finish cooking them on the other side. The cooking time will vary depending on the thickness of the asparagus. For asparagus that is about ½" in diameter, the total cooking time is only about 4 to 5 minutes. It is important not to overcook asparagus. It should still be slightly crisp.

5. Remove the asparagus from the grill and cut it into bite-sized pieces.

6. To make the salsa: in a small bowl, combine the tomatoes, basil, garlic, olive oil, and salt and pepper.

7. Coat a 7" nonstick, oven-safe sauté pan with cooking spray. Heat it over medium heat.

8. In a bowl, lightly beat the eggs or egg whites with a fork until they're slightly frothy. Stir in the asparagus and salt and pepper to taste.

9. Pour the egg mixture into the pan and let it set for about 30 seconds. Transfer it to the oven and bake for about 10 minutes, or until the eggs have just set all the way through and don't jiggle. Remove the frittata from the pan immediately. Remove the frittata to a plate, and spoon the tomato and basil salsa on top.

QUICKIES

- *The best way to remove the frittata from the pan is to place a larger-sized plate directly on top of the pan, then flip it so the frittata drops onto the plate.*

- *The tomato and basil salsa is extremely all-purpose. It would be a great accompaniment to grilled fish, shrimp, scallops, or chicken. Even throw it onto some pasta for a light and fresh topping.*

- *The cooking time differs depending on the thickness of the asparagus. For asparagus that is about ½" in diameter, total cooking time is only about 4 to 5 minutes. It is important not to overcook it. It should still be slightly crisp and maintain a slight crunch.*

Miguel de Cervantes

"All sorrows are less with bread."

starches and pastas
don't worry, they're everyone's weakness

There's no need to be nervous; we eat carbs. Moreover, we won't rat you out on your secret addiction to warm artisan olive and rosemary bread or potatoes au gratin with chives and goat cheese. Your secret is safe with us. However, we have to come clean and simply put it out there: With the good and beautiful comes the mean and ugly.

The average girl is inundated with mixed messages about carbohydrates and their impact on everything from her waistline to the quality of her orgasms. We'll spare you the libido lecture and serve to you as gently as possible what the average girl needs to know about carbohydrates, calories, the low-carb myth, and whole grains. What we will promise you is the following: You don't have to swear off carbs to have a waistline that will have the boys swooning and your mother cooing your praise.

Low-Carb Myth Debunked

You've tried eating healthily to lose weight, but it's just not working. Your mom, dad, sister, next-door neighbor, dry cleaner, and therapist have each lost an average of thirty pounds and are all considering second careers as size-fit models for designer jean labels in Los Angeles. They've all separately recommended you try some variation of the "low-carb diet"—Atkins, South Beach, or "Don't Eat Anything That's White." You're still trying to figure out if that includes marshmallows and Cool Whip. So, you figure it's worth a shot. It seems that's the only way to lose weight.

Hold on, little lady, let's just pause here for a second. We'd like to clear up one major flaw with this thinking: The only thing your body understands is how much energy you're giving it, or in other words, how many calories you're eating. That's right: A calorie is a calorie is a calorie, no matter what the source. That's not to say that some foods aren't more satisfying than others (herb and Stilton–crusted French bread with creamy risotto, but wait, they're *white* . . . foiled again), but a calorie from any source is still a calorie. Your body doesn't know the difference between calories from protein, fat, or carbs.

That doesn't mean, however, that one gram of fat is equal to one gram of carbohydrate or one gram of protein. As luck would have it, a gram of fat is more calorically dense than both a gram of protein and a gram of carbohydrate (that is, one gram of fat has nine calories as opposed to the four calories in a gram of protein or carbohydrate). Surprise!

The truth is that any diet restrictive enough in food choices will cause you to lose weight. This means if your diet consisted of *only* Cool Whip sprinkled with marshmallows, you would lose weight. Now, while that may sound like the best diet in the world, after a week of consuming only those two foods you would most likely go crazy. You did see *Supersize Me*, didn't you? A major cause of overeating, and therefore being overweight, is *too many choices*. Think about what happens when you go to a buffet. You want to try a little of everything, even if you're not all that hungry. Studies have shown that people eat less when there are fewer choices. Take away the huge variety and you'll eat less.

Let's put this in a metaphor that might be more pertinent to your life: *the direct correlation between the activity level of your dating schedule to the availability of Normal, Attractive Men who are Single (NAMS)*. Say, for instance, that the urban or suburban jungle where you reside is like a lush, rich cornucopia bursting with NAMS. In order to determine which NAMS satiate your appetite, you have to eat (that is, date) as many as possible. Over time, the constant sampling from this spread of NAMS will undoubtedly increase a variety of aspects of life.

For starters, your sex life, your confidence, your libido, and perhaps even the clearness of your skin. Now, on the off chance that your town is devoid of NAMS and instead is a fallow playing field chock-full of *Single but Heartless, Unavailable Men who are Self-centered (SHUMS)* then chances are you won't be lining up for that all-you-can-eat buffet. On the upside, you'll lose weight in an instant due to the lack of *choices*!

So, take away variety and choices, as the low-carb diets do, and it makes sense why it works so well. Sure, you can eat seemingly endless bacon, eggs, and cheese, but once you reintroduce cereal, bagels, pretzels, pasta, a few desserts, and a glass of wine, you'll most certainly put the weight back on. Let's all just be honest and state the obvious: We *love* carbs and will eventually reintroduce them into our diets. But by ignoring the real culprits in weight gain—portion control—we're avoiding the true issue at hand.

When the low-carb craze started, it made sense that everyone was losing weight because so many foods were eliminated from the diet. Living in the entrepreneurial and consumer-centric country we live in, it was not long before the food industry capitalized on this latest fad. America conceived the "net carb." The net carb's claim to fame is that only certain carbohydrates increase blood sugar. These spikes in blood sugar lead to overeating (because post sugar-spike comes the inevitable low, the jitters, and eventually the hunger that comes along with it). Net carbs are calculated by subtracting grams of fiber and grams of sugar alcohol from the total grams of carbohydrate. In reality, however, net carbs have no real definition. It is a term *fabricated* by the food industry.

And, despite what the food industry would like us to believe, those grams of fiber and sugar alcohol still count. In reality, low-carb foods are generally higher in fat and protein and often have the same number of calories as the regular product. And, now that there are so many low-carb cookies, pastas, chocolates, and other products available, there is once again variety for those following a low-carb diet.

As a result, all those people who were originally having so much success with these diets no longer find that to be the case. Again, back to our NAMS vs. SHUMS metaphor: The addition of NAMS to the market lends itself to you eating (dating) more. It all comes back to the fact that any diet that is restrictive in food groups will cause you to lose weight. If you add choices back into the equation, these diets no longer work.

At the end of the day, a calorie is a calorie, and in order to lose weight you need to take in fewer calories than you expend. While a calorie may be a calorie and net carbs may be a conspiracy, the truth is that not all carbohydrates are created equal. The wide world of whole grains awaits you.

The Complete Package: Whole Grains

How many times in your life has your Grandmother squeezed your face and said, "Honey, bubeleh, sweetness, mi vida, you need to find yourself the perfect man, the complete package. It's time for you to settle down." Once a week, once a month, every other full moon? Enough times that you've considered fabricating an entire relationship just to keep her and your family at bay?

Each time you engage in forced family fun (Sunday night dinner, high holidays, 4th of July barbecues, Easter brunch), you know what everyone at the table is thinking: "When is she going to provide us with grandchildren?" Each time you return home, you contemplate harvesting your eggs, as you're certain the "perfect guy" does not exist—he is the latest conspiracy theory foisted upon us by the retail wedding industry. He's a contrived deity propelling you to register at Crate and Barrel, Williams-Sonoma, and Bloomingdale's! You know you're only buying time. Your family has a point: You just need to suck it up and find the perfect guy.

Eating whole grains is like finding the perfect guy. So, how is this correlation even remotely helpful to your chances of getting married and conceiving children before your viable eggs shrivel up? Here's the thought:

Whole grains provide fiber, vitamin E, selenium, potassium, magnesium, and other nutrients.

The perfect guy provides fiber (stable income and health insurance), vitamin E (access to a vacation home in Palm Beach, Jackson Hole, and/or Maui), selenium (a propensity to shower you with jewelry on random occasions), potassium (a mother whom you could adore), magnesium (ridiculous genetic potential such that you are itching to procreate), and many other wonderful attributes.

Whole grains contain all three parts of the grain—bran, germ, and endosperm.

The perfect guy comprises all three parts of manhood—brawn, brain, and sperm.

Other grains, also referred to as refined grains, have had at least one or more of the parts of the grain removed. Therefore, they have little or no fiber, less protein, and little to no antioxidants. Basically, they're playing with half a deck.

Other guys, also referred to as genetic liabilities to your unborn children, have been damaged by one or more of the following: their mother, their ex-girlfriend(s), their inflated ego (due to the above first mentioned), their deflated ego (as a result of the above second mentioned).

We've outlined why it's just as important to make the distinction between whole grains and refined grains as it is to differentiate between the "perfect guy" and the "genetic liability." Now, it's imperative that you incorporate the following measures to increase whole grains in your diet. A few sources of whole grains:

Whole wheat	*Quinoa*
Oats	*Millet*
Corn	*Bulgur*
Barley	*Amaranth*
Whole rye	*Brown rice*
Buckwheat	

As many of you have experienced, landmines abound in the hunt for the "perfect guy." We like to refer to him as "the decoy." He's the one who claims to be the amazing, attentive, supportive, intelligent, and loyal guy, but in actuality is a genetic liability in disguise. Beware. They are all around you.

Similarly, how will you know if something is a whole grain? Specifically, look for the word "whole" on the ingredient list. Much like the decoy man, many breads and crackers use tan coloring to mimic whole wheat but are, in fact, not whole wheat. Therefore, you should always

> **Food Swaps:**
> **Increase Your *Whole* Grain Intake**
>
> | Out with the Old | In with the New |
> |---|---|
> | Sugar cereal | Oatmeal |
> | Bagel | Whole-wheat English muffin |
> | Wheat bread | Whole-wheat bread |
> | Sweetened granola bar | Kashi bar or High-Fiber Bar |
> | Potato chips | Air-popped popcorn |
> | White pasta | Whole-wheat pasta |
> | French bread | Whole rye bread |

reference the ingredient list and confirm they list "whole wheat" or some other whole grain and *not* "wheat flour." Wheat flour is not a whole grain.

Let's talk numbers and get down to the nitty gritty. Here are the basics:

1. Ideally, the whole grain should be the first or second ingredient in the ingredient list.
2. Most women need about five to seven servings of grains each day, and at least half of those should be whole grains. A serving is equal to:
   - *1 slice of bread (i.e., store-bought bread)*
   - *½ English muffin*
   - *¼ bagel*
   - *5 whole-wheat crackers*
   - *1 small tortilla (4 ounce)*
   - *¾ cup dry cereal (except granola)*
   - *¼ cup granola*
   - *½ cup cooked rice (white, brown, or wild; brown or wild are healthier since they are whole grains)*
   - *½ cup cooked pasta*
   - *½ cup hot cereal, cooked*
   - *½ hot dog bun or hamburger roll*
   - *3 plain rice cakes*
   - *1 pack nonflavored instant oatmeal*
   - *3 cups light (unbuttered) popcorn*

Simple changes to your diet to include more whole grains include:

- Eat a cereal such as oatmeal.
- Make a sandwich with whole-wheat bread.
- Start your day off with a whole-wheat English muffin with peanut butter.
- Substitute your afternoon scone from Starbucks with air-popped popcorn or whole-wheat crackers.
- Introduce wild rice to your dinner in place of potatoes, white rice, and Wonder bread.

Herbed Root Vegetable Mash

1. Chop the parsnip, rutabaga, and potato into equal-sized cubes, about ½".

2. Add the veggies to a pot of salted water. Bring to a boil and boil them until tender enough to mash. A fork or knife should slip in easily and have no resistance when pulled out. Drain them well in a colander, return them to the pot, and let them dry out over low heat for 1 minute.

3. With a fork or a masher, mash the veggies until your desired consistency. (A few lumps won't kill you.)

4. Stir in the butter, milk, parsley, thyme, salt, and pepper.

5. Add more milk if the mash seems too thick.

QUICKIES

- *Parsnips are white root vegetables that look similar to carrots. They have a smooth, sweet flavor and should not be discolored or dried out. You can refrigerate parsnips in a plastic bag for up to 2 weeks.*

- *Italian flat-leaf parsley has much better flavor than curly parsley. It's usually next to curly parsley in the grocery store, and, yes, it has flat leaves, which are pretty easy to distinguish.*

- *To chop herbs, gather them up into a bundle together and chop with a chef's knife.*

NUTRIENTS
Antioxidants
Calcium
Fiber
Folate

1 small parsnip, peeled

1 small rutabaga, peeled

1 small potato, peeled

1 teaspoon butter or butter spray

3 to 4 tablespoons non-fat milk

2 teaspoons chopped fresh Italian flat-leaf parsley

1 teaspoon chopped fresh thyme (leaves only, no stems)

Salt and pepper to taste

COOKING ACCESSORIES
Vegetable peeler
Chef's knife
2-Quart pot
Colander
Potato masher

Herb and Garlic Roasted New Potatoes

NUTRIENTS
Antioxidants
Fiber
Folate

¼ pound baby new potatoes (approximately 4 or 5)

1 to 2 cloves garlic, thinly sliced

Salt and pepper to taste

½ tablespoon extra-virgin olive oil

1 teaspoon chopped fresh Italian flat-leaf parsley

½ teaspoon chopped fresh rosemary (leaves only, no stems)

½ teaspoon chopped fresh thyme (leaves only, no stems)

COOKING ACCESSORIES

Chef's knife

8" × 8" Baking pan or other small baking dish

Aluminum foil

1. Heat the oven to 500°F.

2. Rinse and pat dry the potatoes, and cut into halves or quarters, depending on their size. The pieces should all be around the same size to ensure that their cooking time is equal.

3. In a baking dish, combine the potatoes, garlic, salt, pepper, and enough olive oil to coat the potatoes. Cover the dish tightly with foil.

4. Roast for 40 minutes, or until potatoes are fork-tender but not mushy.

5. Toss the hot potatoes with the herbs in the baking dish.

QUICKIES

- *You can substitute any potato you like—russets (cut into chunks), Yukon golds, fingerlings, Peruvian blues, creamers, or white, just to name a few.*

- *To chop herbs, gather them up into a bundle together and chop with a chef's knife.*

- *To get rid of the scent of garlic from your hands, slice a lemon in half and rub it all over. The acid in the juice helps remove the odor.*

Roasted New Potato Salad

1. Heat a 7" sauté pan over medium high heat and coat it with the olive oil.

2. When the pan and oil are hot, add the corn and sauté until slightly browned, about 3 to 4 minutes.

3. In a mixing bowl, combine the potatoes, peppers, corn, olives, vinaigrette, salt, and pepper; mix well.

QUICKIES

- *During the summer when corn is at its peak, use fresh. Otherwise, frozen corn is a great option. Frozen corn is picked at its prime, then frozen immediately so you can get ripe, sweet corn all year long.*

- *We recommend buying roasted red peppers in a jar rather than taking the time to roast your own.*

- *You can substitute any potato you like—russets (cut into chunks), Yukon golds, fingerlings, Peruvian blues, creamers, or white, just to name a few.*

NUTRIENTS
Antioxidants
Fiber
Folate
Whole Grain

1 teaspoon extra-virgin olive oil

¼ cup frozen corn

1 finished recipe for Herb and Garlic Roasted New Potatoes (recipe precedes)

2 tablespoons sliced roasted red bell peppers

1 tablespoon coarsely chopped pitted kalamata olives

2 tablespoons Balsamic-Herb Vinaigrette (page 227)

Salt and pepper to taste

COOKING ACCESSORIES
Chef's knife

8" × 8" Baking pan

Aluminum foil

7" Sauté pan

Whisk

Bowl

Chinese Five-Spice Sweet Potato Oven Fries

½ tablespoon light extra-virgin olive oil

1½ tablespoons Chinese five-spice powder

1 tablespoon brown sugar

Salt and pepper to taste

1 small sweet potato, about ¼ pound, cut into ¾" wedges

1. Heat the oven to 400°F.

2. Combine the olive oil, five-spice powder, brown sugar, salt, and pepper in a bowl.

3. Add the sweet potato wedges and toss to coat evenly.

4. Place the sweet potatoes in an oven-safe dish and bake for 20 to 25 minutes, or until the potatoes are fork-tender but not mushy.

QUICKIE

- *Found on the spice aisle of your grocery store, Chinese five-spice powder is a blend of cinnamon, cloves, fennel seed, star anise, and Szechuan peppercorns.*

COOKING ACCESSORIES

Chef's knife

Bowl

8" × 8" Baking pan or other small baking dish

Couscous with Apricots and Smokey Almonds

1. Bring the chicken broth to a boil in a 1-quart pot.

2. Add the couscous and cinnamon, stir, and cover with foil or a lid. Turn off the heat.

3. Let the couscous sit for 5 minutes.

4. Fluff the couscous with a fork, breaking up all of the grains.

5. Stir in the butter until melted.

6. Add the apricots, almonds, parsley, and salt and stir to combine.

QUICKIES

- *Though couscous looks like a grain, it's actually tiny pasta made from semolina flour. It's very versatile and originally hails from Northern Africa.*

- *Italian flat-leaf parsley has much better flavor than curly parsley. It's usually next to curly parsley in the grocery store, and, yes, it has flat leaves, which are pretty easy to distinguish.*

NUTRIENTS
Antioxidants
Fiber*
Whole Grain*
*High-fiber and whole-grain only if whole-wheat couscous is used.

⅓ cup low-sodium chicken broth

⅓ cup couscous

Pinch cinnamon

½ teaspoon butter or butter spray

1 tablespoon chopped dried apricots

1 tablespoon smoked almonds (or regular almonds if you prefer)

1 tablespoon chopped fresh Italian flat-leaf parsley

Salt to taste

COOKING ACCESSORIES
Chef's knife
1-Quart pot with a lid, or foil

Couscous Tabbouleh

½ cup water

½ cup couscous

½ cup chopped cucumber (peel if not using an English or hothouse cucumber)

½ small tomato, chopped

½ scallion or green onion, thinly sliced. Use both the green and white parts, but trim off the root.

2 tablespoons chopped fresh Italian flat-leaf parsley

1 tablespoon chopped fresh mint (leaves only, no stems)

Juice of half a lemon

1 teaspoon extra-virgin olive oil

Salt and pepper to taste

COOKING ACCESSORIES

Chef's knife

1-Quart pot with a lid, or foil

Bowl

1. In a 1-quart pot, bring the water to a boil.

2. Stir in the couscous, remove the pan from the heat, and cover the pan tightly with the lid or foil.

3. Let the pan sit for 5 minutes.

4. Fluff the couscous with a fork so that there are no lumps, and let it cool completely.

5. In a bowl, combine the couscous with the cucumber, tomato, scallion, parsley, mint, lemon juice, olive oil, salt, and pepper. Mix well.

QUICKIES

- *Tabbouleh is a salad commonly found in Greece and other Mediterranean locales. Traditionally made with a grain called bulgur, this couscous version is a speedier version than its bulgur predecessor.*

- *Though couscous looks like a grain, it's actually tiny pasta made from semolina flour. It's very versatile and originally hails from Northern Africa.*

- *To chop herbs, gather them up into a bundle together and chop with a chef's knife.*

Coconut-Ginger Jasmine Rice

1. Bring the coconut milk and water to a boil in a 1-quart pot.

2. Add the rice and stir.

3. When the water returns to a boil, cover the pan with both foil and a lid. Lower the heat to low and cook for 15 minutes.

4. Fluff the rice using a fork. Stir in the ginger, scallion, salt, and pepper.

QUICKIES

- *In general, when cooking rice the ratio of water to rice is 2 to 1. Brown rice requires more water, so check the package instructions.*

- *The best way to peel ginger is with a spoon. Yes, a spoon. Also, instead of chopping it, you can use a microplane to finely grate it.*

NUTRIENTS
Antioxidants
Calcium

⅓ cup light coconut milk

⅓ cup water

⅓ cup jasmine rice

½" piece of fresh ginger (about 1 teaspoon), peeled and finely minced (or grated with a microplane)

¼ scallion or green onion, chopped. Use both the white and green parts, but remember to trim off the root.

Salt and pepper to taste

COOKING ACCESSORIES
Microplane (optional)
Chef's knife
1-Quart pot with a lid
Aluminum foil

Wild Rice with Sweet Corn and Scallions

NUTRIENTS
Antioxidants
Fiber
Folate
Whole Grain

1 quart water

⅓ cup wild rice

1 teaspoon butter

¼ cup frozen corn

½ scallion or green onion, thinly
  sliced. Use both the green and
  white parts, but remember to trim
  off the root.

Salt and pepper to taste

COOKING ACCESSORIES

2-Quart pot

Colander

7" Sauté pan

Chef's knife

Bowl

1. Bring 1 quart of water to a boil in a 2-quart pot. Boil the rice as you would boil pasta (uncovered), until tender but not mushy, about 30 minutes. Some of the grains will have burst open during cooking. If the water begins to dry out, just add more. Drain the rice well in a colander and return it to the pot.

2. Meanwhile, heat a 7" sauté pan over medium high heat. Coat it with the butter. When the pan is hot, add the corn and sauté until slightly golden, about 5 minutes.

3. In a small bowl, combine the rice with the corn, scallion, salt, and pepper and stir well.

QUICKIE

- *Wild rice is actually a grain. Cook wild rice the same way as you would cook pasta. Boil it in a lot of water until it's tender, then drain.*

Citrus Basmati Rice

1. Bring the water to a boil in a 1-quart pot. Stir in the rice and bring back to a boil.

2. Cover the pan with both foil and a lid. Reduce the heat and simmer on low for 15 minutes, or until all the water is absorbed.

3. Fluff the rice with a fork.

4. Add and stir in the lemon and orange zest, salt, pepper, and butter (if using).

QUICKIES

- Basmati *literally translates as "queen of fragrance." This type of rice originally comes from the Himalayas and has a delicate perfume and flavor.*

- *Instantly convert this into a low-fat recipe by omitting the butter.*

- *The easiest way to zest a lemon is to use a microplane. Just be careful to remove only the yellow part of the skin because the white pith is very bitter. If you don't have a microplane, you can peel the skin off using a vegetable peeler and finely chop it with a knife.*

NUTRIENTS

Antioxidants   Low-fat**
Fiber*   Whole Grain*

*High-fiber and whole-grain only if brown rice is used.

**Low-fat only if made without butter.

⅔ cup water
⅓ cup basmati rice
¼ teaspoon lemon zest
¼ teaspoon orange zest
Salt and pepper to taste
1 teaspoon butter (optional)

COOKING ACCESSORIES

1-Quart pot with a lid
Aluminum foil
Microplane

Rice Pilaf

NUTRIENTS
Antioxidants
Folate

1 teaspoon extra-virgin olive oil

1 shallot, chopped

⅓ cup long-grain rice

Salt and pepper to taste

⅔ cup chicken broth or water

COOKING ACCESSORIES

1-Quart pot with a lid

Chef's knife

Wooden spoon or heat-resistant spatula

Aluminum foil

1. Heat the olive oil in a 1-quart pot.

2. When the pot and oil are hot, add the shallot and cook until translucent.

3. Stir in the rice and let it toast for about a minute, stirring occasionally with a wooden spoon or heat-resistant spatula.

4. Add the salt, pepper, and broth or water.

5. Bring to a boil, cover with both foil and a lid, and reduce the heat to low. Let the rice simmer for 15 minutes.

6. Remove the pan from the heat and fluff the rice with a fork.

QUICKIES

- *Pilaf is actually just a method, so the method shown here can be used for any kind of rice—use your favorite. It's great just like this, or add herbs, olives, nuts, etc.*

- *Cooking shallots and onions until translucent means until they become see-through. If the pan is too hot, they will caramelize instead, so turn the heat down if necessary. Caramelizing imparts a much different flavor.*

Orzo with Grilled Asparagus, Sweet Peas, and Parmesan

1. Cook the orzo according to the package instructions. Make sure to add ½ teaspoon salt to the water before adding the pasta. Drain the orzo well in a colander.

2. Cut the asparagus into bite-sized pieces. Heat a 7" sauté pan over medium heat, add olive oil, and heat the asparagus and olives in the skillet.

3. Add in the cooked pasta, frozen peas, Parmesan cheese, and salt and pepper. Cook until heated through.

4. Transfer the pasta to a bowl and sprinkle it with parsley and basil.

QUICKIES

- *Adding salt to the water in which the pasta is cooked is very important because it is the only opportunity to season the pasta. Otherwise, it won't have any flavor.*

- *To chop herbs, gather them up into a bundle together and chop with a chef's knife.*

NUTRIENTS
Antioxidants
Calcium
Fiber
Folate
Whole Grain

⅓ cup whole-wheat orzo

½ teaspoon salt

3 to 5 asparagus spears, cooked according to Grilled Asparagus with Fresh Lemon and Olives (page 76)

1 teaspoon extra-virgin olive oil

2 tablespoons frozen sweet peas

1 tablespoon grated Parmesan cheese

Salt and pepper to taste

1 teaspoon chopped Italian flat-leaf parsley

1 teaspoon chopped fresh basil (leaves only, no stems)

COOKING ACCESSORIES
Chef's knife

Tongs

2-Quart pot

7" Sauté pan

Colander

Angel Hair with Basil Pesto, Grape Tomatoes, and Pine Nuts

NUTRIENTS
Antioxidants
Calcium
Fiber
Folate
Whole Grain

BASIL PESTO:

1 cup fresh basil leaves (stems removed), packed

1 tablespoon pine nuts, toasted

¼ cup grated Parmesan cheese

1 clove garlic, chopped (or use a garlic press)

¼ cup extra-virgin olive oil

Juice of half a lemon

Salt and pepper to taste

Combine all the pesto ingredients in a food processor or blender and blend until smooth. If you're using a blender, you'll probably need to add a little more oil for it to blend well.

QUICKIES

- *Angel hair is ideal for a quick meal because it is so thin that it takes only a few minutes to cook. If you have basil pesto stored in your freezer, you can have this meal done in 5 minutes.*

- *Toast nuts on a baking sheet in a 300°F oven for just a few minutes. They are done cooking as soon as you can smell them. Overcooking them will burn their oils and they'll become bitter. You can also toast them in a dry pan (without oil) on the stove; toss them occasionally.*

COOKING ACCESSORIES

Garlic press (optional)

Food processor or blender

Chef's knife or serrated knife

2-Quart pot

Colander

TO FINISH:

1. Cook the angel hair according to the package instructions. Make sure to add ½ teaspoon salt to the water before adding the pasta. Drain the pasta well in a colander and return it to the pot.

2. Stir in the pesto, tomatoes, and pine nuts.

TO FINISH DISH:

2 to 3 ounces whole-wheat angel hair

½ teaspoon salt

¼ Basil Pesto, about 2 tablespoons, (recipe precedes, freeze the balance)

¼ cup grape tomatoes, halved

½ tablespoon pine nuts, toasted

Angel Hair with Mushroom Ragout

MUSHROOM RAGOUT (WHOLE RECIPE):

1 tablespoon butter or extra-virgin olive oil

3 cups assorted mushrooms (e.g., button, portobello, shiitake), sliced into ¼" pieces

1 shallot, chopped

Salt and pepper to taste

1 clove garlic, chopped (or use a garlic press)

2 tablespoons white wine (or sherry or Madeira)

1 teaspoon chopped fresh thyme (leaves only, no stems)

COOKING ACCESSORIES

Chef's knife

Garlic press (optional)

10" (or larger) skillet

Wooden spoon or heat-resistant spatula

2-Quart pot

Colander

1. Melt the butter or pour the olive oil in a 10" skillet over medium high heat.

2. When the pan is hot, add the mushrooms, shallot, salt, and pepper and sauté for about 5 minutes, or until the mushrooms begin to soften and most of the moisture that comes out of the mushrooms evaporates.

3. Add the garlic and cook until fragrant (only 10 seconds or so).

4. Add the wine and scrape up any browned bits from the bottom of the pan using a wooden spoon or heat-resistant spatula. Let the wine cook down and evaporate until the pan is almost dry. Stir in the thyme.

QUICKIES

- *Almost any type of pasta can be used in this recipe, so feel free to just use what you have.*

- *Choose your favorite mushrooms for this. Most markets these days have a large variety of both wild and cultivated mushrooms. Wild mushrooms include chantarelle, shiitake, oyster, and porcini. Cultivated includes white button, crimini (which are baby portobellos), and portobellos.*

- *Shallots are similar to onions but have a more delicate, sweeter flavor. You can find them in your grocery store next to onions, or sometimes near the garlic. They're perfect for meals-for-one because they are much smaller than onions.*

Angel Hair with Mushroom Ragout (cont'd)

TO FINISH:

1. Cook the angel hair according to the package instructions. Make sure to add ½ teaspoon salt to the water before adding the pasta. Drain the pasta well in a colander.

2. If the mushroom ragout is left over from another recipe, heat it in a medium-large skillet over medium heat. Add the pasta to the hot ragout and combine well.

3. Top the pasta with Parmesan cheese.

TO FINISH DISH:

2 to 3 ounces whole-wheat angel hair

½ teaspoon salt

½ recipe Mushroom Ragout (recipe precedes)

1 tablespoon grated Parmesan cheese

Baked Penne with Turkey Bolognese and Ricotta

TURKEY BOLOGNESE:

1 teaspoon extra-virgin olive oil

½ onion, diced

1 clove garlic, minced (or use a garlic press)

2 teaspoons chopped fresh oregano (leaves only, no stems)

¼ pound lean ground turkey (check the package to be sure it says "lean")

½ cup store-bought tomato sauce, or Basic Tomato Sauce (page 230)

Salt and pepper to taste

COOKING ACCESSORIES

Chef's knife

Garlic press (optional)

10" Skillet with lid

Wooden spoon or
heat-resistant spatula

2-Quart pot

Colander

9" × 5" Loaf pan or 8" × 8" baking pan

MAKES 2 TO 3 SERVINGS

1. Heat the oven to 350°F.

2. Heat a 10" skillet over medium heat and add the olive oil. When the pan is heated, add the onion and cook until translucent. Add the garlic and oregano and cook for 30 seconds.

3. Raise heat to high. Add the ground turkey and cook it until browned, breaking up any large chunks with a wooden spoon or heat-resistant spatula. Add the tomato sauce and simmer for 15 minutes. If it gets too dry, add a little more tomato sauce and cover with a lid. Season with salt and pepper.

Baked Penne (cont'd)

TO FINISH:

1. Cook the penne according to the package instructions. Make sure to add ½ teaspoon salt to the water before adding the pasta. Drain the penne well in a colander.

2. Toss the penne with the ricotta and Bolognese sauce.

3. Spray an oven-safe dish (9" × 5" loaf pan or 8" × 8" baking pan) with nonstick spray. Pour in the penne mixture in an even layer and top with Parmesan cheese. Bake until bubbly, about 30 minutes.

QUICKIE

When following the cooking instructions for the penne, cook it for about 2 minutes less because it will cook again in the oven. This will prevent the pasta from overcooking and becoming mushy.

TO FINISH DISH:

¾ cup whole-wheat penne

½ teaspoon salt

4 tablespoons low-fat or nonfat ricotta cheese

1 to 2 tablespoons shredded Parmesan cheese

Fusilli with Turkey Italian Sausage, Green Peas, and Mozzarella

¾ cup whole-wheat fusilli

½ teaspoon salt

1 teaspoon extra-virgin olive oil

1 link turkey Italian sausage, sliced into ½" rounds, then cut into half moons

2 shallots, sliced

2 tablespoons frozen sweet green peas

2 tablespoons shredded part-skim mozzarella cheese; if using fresh, cut into ½" cubes

Salt and pepper to taste

Crushed red chili flakes (optional)

COOKING ACCESSORIES

Chef's knife

10" Skillet

2-Quart pot

Colander

Wooden spoon or heat-resistant spatula

1. Cook the fusilli according to the package instructions. Make sure to add ½ teaspoon salt to the water before adding the pasta. Drain the fusilli well in a colander.

2. Heat a 10" skillet over medium heat and add the olive oil. When the pan is hot, add the sausage and shallots. Cook until the sausage browns and the shallots are translucent.

3. Add the hot pasta to the skillet, along with the peas, cheese, salt, pepper, and chili flakes (if using). Toss well.

QUICKIES

- *Cooking shallots and onions until translucent means until they become see-through. If the pan is too hot they will caramelize instead, so turn the heat down if necessary. Caramelizing imparts a much different flavor.*

- *Buy sausage that is already cooked to cut down on your time in the kitchen.*

- *Sausage typically comes prepackaged in sets of five. Use one for this recipe and freeze the leftover four in freezer-safe zip-top bags.*

Linguine with Garlicky Steamed Mussels

1. Heat a 7" sauté pan over medium heat and coat it with the olive oil.

2. When the pan and oil are heated, add the garlic and red pepper flakes and cook about 1 minute. Take care not to brown the garlic or it will become bitter.

3. Add the wine, lemon juice, clam juice or broth, and mussels.

4. Cover with a lid and cook 2 to 3 minutes, or until all of the mussels have opened, discarding any that have not.

TO FINISH:

1. Cook the linguine according to the package instructions. Make sure to add ½ teaspoon salt to the water before adding the pasta. Drain the linguine well in a colander.

2. Top the linguine with the mussels, and sprinkle with parsley.

QUICKIES

- *Clams can be substituted for the mussels for a more classic dish.*

- *If, when cleaning mussels, you come across an open one, give it a squeeze. If it closes up, it's good; if not, discard it.*

NUTRIENTS
Antioxidants
Fiber
Folate
Omega-3
Whole Grain

GARLICKY STEAMED MUSSELS:

½ tablespoon extra-virgin olive oil
1 clove garlic, thinly sliced
¼ teaspoon crushed red pepper flakes
2 tablespoons dry white wine
Juice of half a lemon
¼ cup clam juice or vegetable broth
¼ pound mussels, scrubbed well
2 teaspoons chopped parsley

TO FINISH DISH:

2 to 3 ounces Whole Grain linguine
½ teaspoon salt
1 recipe Garlicky Steamed Mussels
Crushed red chili flakes (optional)

COOKING ACCESSORIES

Chef's knife
7" Sauté pan with lid
2-Quart pot
Colander

Linguine with Scampi-Style Shrimp

SCAMPI-STYLE SHRIMP:

½ tablespoon extra-virgin olive oil

1 clove garlic, chopped (or use a garlic press)

1 tablespoon white wine or sherry

¼ pound medium-sized shrimp, peeled and de-veined

Salt and pepper to taste

½ tablespoon chopped fresh Italian flat-leaf parsley

¼ teaspoon crushed red chili flakes (optional)

COOKING ACCESSORIES

Chef's knife

Paring knife to de-vein shrimp

7" sauté pan

2-quart pot

Colander

Tongs

1. Heat a 7" sauté pan over medium heat and coat it with the olive oil.

2. When the pan is heated, add the garlic and cook until fragrant, about 30 seconds.

3. Add the wine and let it reduce (boil down) by half.

4. Season the shrimp with salt and pepper on both sides and add it to the pan. Cook it for about 1 minute per side, or until just pink. Do not overcook or the shrimp will become rubbery.

5. Stir in the parsley, and the chili flakes if desired.

QUICKIES

- *An easy way to cut down on carbs but still feel satisfied is to add more shrimp while cutting back on the pasta. You'll still get your pasta fix without going overboard.*

- *You can buy shrimp that have already been peeled and de-veined. To do it yourself, twist off the tail and peel the shell off, making sure to remove all of the legs. To de-vein, run a paring knife along the back of the shrimp (the opposite side from where the legs were) just deep enough to expose the vein. The vein can range from a dark color to translucent. Pull it out with the tip of the knife.*

Linguine with Scampi-Style Shrimp (cont'd)

TO FINISH:

1. Cook the linguine according to the package instructions. Make sure to add ½ teaspoon salt to the water before adding the pasta. Drain well in a colander.

2. Toss the linguine together with the shrimp, using tongs, and squeeze lemon juice on top.

TO FINISH DISH:

2 to 3 ounces whole-wheat linguine

½ teaspoon salt

1 recipe Scampi-Style Shrimp, as precedes

Juice of a quarter of a lemon

Orzo with Roasted Chicken, Black Olives and Sun-Dried Tomatoes

⅓ cup whole-wheat orzo

½ teaspoon salt

½ chicken breast from Whole Roasted Chicken recipe (page 112), cut into chunks

½ tablespoon roughly chopped pitted kalamata olives

½ tablespoon sliced sun-dried tomatoes (about 1 sun-dried tomato)

Juice of a quarter lemon

Zest of half a lemon

1 teaspoon extra-virgin olive oil

Salt and pepper to taste

1 teaspoon chopped Italian flat-leaf parsley

COOKING ACCESSORIES

2-Quart pot

Chef's knife

Microplane

Colander

Bowl

1. Cook the orzo according to the package instructions. Make sure to add ½ teaspoon salt to the water before adding the pasta. Drain the orzo well in a colander.

2. Combine the orzo, chicken, olives, sun-dried tomatoes, lemon juice, lemon zest, olive oil, salt and pepper, and parsley in a bowl. Gently stir until blended.

QUICKIES

- *An easy way to save calories is to buy sun-dried tomatoes that are packed in water instead of olive oil. In some stores you can also buy them loose, which will save you some casholah, and you can store them in your fridge just fine.*

- *This is a great version of pasta salad and can be eaten warm or at room temperature.*

- *The easiest way to zest a lemon is to use a microplane. Just be careful to remove only the yellow part of the skin because the white pith is very bitter. If you don't have a microplane, you can peel the skin off using a vegetable peeler and finely chop it with a knife.*

Penne with Beans and Greens

1. Heat a 10" skillet over medium heat and add the olive oil. When the pan is hot, add the shallots and cook until translucent. Add the garlic and beans with their reserved liquid and cook about 1 to 2 minutes or until the beans are hot.

2. Add the spinach and lemon zest. Toss the spinach, using tongs, until it is wilted but not brown. This only takes a minute, so be careful not to overcook the spinach. Season the spinach with salt and pepper to taste.

3. Cook the penne according to the package instructions. Make sure to add ½ teaspoon salt to the water before adding the pasta. Using a slotted spoon, remove the pasta from the water and add it to the spinach mixture; toss to combine. Add some of the remaining pasta water if it needs a little more moisture.

4. Top the pasta with Parmesan.

QUICKIES

- *Frozen spinach will work in this recipe. Just make sure to defrost and squeeze all of the excess moisture out of it so you don't have a watery dish at the end.*

- *Cooking shallots and onions until translucent means until they become see-through. If the pan is too hot they will caramelize instead, so turn the heat down if necessary. Caramelizing imparts a much different flavor.*

NUTRIENTS
Antioxidants
Calcium
Fiber
Folate
Whole Grain

---

1 teaspoon extra-virgin olive oil

¾ cup whole-wheat penne

½ teaspoon salt

1 shallot, sliced

1 clove garlic, minced

3 tablespoons canned white beans (cannellini or Great Northern beans), plus 2 tablespoons of the liquid

2 cups fresh spinach

Zest of half a lemon, about ½ teaspoon

Salt and pepper to taste

1 tablespoon grated Parmesan cheese

COOKING ACCESSORIES
10" Skillet

Chef's knife

Garlic press (optional)

Microplane

Tongs

2-Quart pot

Slotted spoon

Spaghetti with Basic Tomato Sauce and Shaved Parmesan Cheese

NUTRIENTS
Antioxidants
Fiber
Folate
Whole Grain

BASIC TOMATO SAUCE:

1 tablespoon extra-virgin olive oil

½ small onion, diced

2 cloves garlic, minced (or use a garlic press)

¼ bunch roughly chopped fresh basil (leaves only, no stems), about ⅓ to ½ cup

1 (14-ounce) can crushed tomatoes

Salt and pepper to taste

COOKING ACCESSORIES

Chef's knife

Garlic press (optional)

1-Quart saucepan

Wooden spoon or heat-resistant spatula

2-Quart pot

Colander

10" Skillet if reheating sauce

Vegetable peeler

MAKES ABOUT 2 CUPS

1. Heat a 1-quart pot over medium heat and add the olive oil.

2. When the pan is hot, add the onion and cook about 4 minutes, or until soft and translucent but not browned, stirring with a wooden spoon or heat-resistant spatula.

3. Add the garlic and cook about 1 minute.

4. Add the basil and tomatoes. Bring to a boil, then reduce the heat to low, cover, and simmer 15 to 30 minutes, stirring occasionally.

5. Season the sauce with salt and pepper.

QUICKIES

- *Buy a block of Parmesan cheese and use a vegetable peeler to create shavings. You won't use much cheese but it can be stored, tightly wrapped, in the freezer.*

- *Cooking shallots and onions until translucent means until they become see-through. If the pan is too hot they will caramelize instead, so turn the heat down if necessary. Caramelizing imparts a much different flavor.*

- *To get rid of the scent of garlic from your hands, slice a lemon in half and rub it all over. The acid in the juice helps remove the odor.*

Spaghetti with Basic Tomato Sauce (cont'd)

TO FINISH:

1. Cook the spaghetti according to the package instructions. Make sure to add ½ teaspoon salt to the water before adding the pasta. Drain the spaghetti well in a colander.

2. If you're using sauce you've previously made, reheat it in a large skillet, add the spaghetti, and toss together. Otherwise, return the spaghetti to the pot you cooked it in, add the hot sauce, and stir to combine.

3. Top the spaghetti with Parmesan shavings.

TO FINISH DISH:

2 to 3 ounces whole-wheat spaghetti (a little smaller than the diameter of the neck of a wine bottle)

¼ to ½ cup Basic Tomato Sauce recipe (recipe precedes)

5 shavings Parmesan cheese

Spaghetti with Sun-Dried Tomato Pesto and Baby Broccoli

SUN-DRIED TOMATO PESTO:

½ cup sun-dried tomatoes packed in olive oil, drained well

1 tablespoon toasted almonds

1 small clove garlic, chopped (or use a garlic press)

2 tablespoons grated Parmesan cheese

1 teaspoon fresh lemon juice (juice of about half a lemon)

Salt and pepper to taste

COOKING ACCESSORIES

Food processor

2-quart pot

Chef's knife

Colander

1-quart pot

Tongs

MAKES ABOUT ½ CUP

Combine all ingredients in a food processor or blender. Blend until smooth, about 15 to 20 seconds.

QUICKIES

- *Make the pesto ahead of time and store it in the fridge for up to 5 days, or keep it in the freezer longer. To freeze it in individual servings, put it into an ice cube tray and pop out one "cube" per meal.*

- *Toast nuts on a baking sheet in a 300°F oven for just a few minutes. They are done cooking as soon as you can smell them. Overcooking them will burn their oils and they'll become bitter. You can also toast them in a dry pan (without oil) on the stove; toss them occasionally.*

Spaghetti with Sun-Dried Tomato Pesto (cont'd)

TO FINISH:

1. Cook the spaghetti according to the package instructions. Make sure to add ½ teaspoon salt to the water before adding the pasta. Drain the spaghetti well in a colander and return it to the pot.

2. Bring a 2-quart pot of water to a boil. Trim off any ends of the broccoli that look dried out or discolored. Boil the broccoli for about 3 minutes, or until the stalks are tender but not mushy. Drain the broccoli well in a colander.

3. With tongs, toss the hot pasta with the pesto, broccoli, salt, pepper, and parsley.

TO FINISH DISH:

2 to 3 ounces whole-wheat spaghetti (a handful that's a little smaller than the diameter of the neck of a wine bottle)

½ teaspoon salt

½ recipe Sun-Dried Tomato Pesto (recipe precedes)

½ cup baby broccoli (about 3 or 4 stalks)

Salt and pepper to taste

2 teaspoons chopped Italian flat-leaf parsley

Pizza Dough

NUTRIENTS
Folate
Low-fat

1 cup warm water

¾ teaspoon active dry yeast

2 cups all-purpose flour or bread flour, plus more for kneading

¾ teaspoon salt

Cooking spray

COOKING ACCESSORIES

Large bowl

Whisk

Food processor, if using

Damp dish towel

Rolling pin (or the side of a wine bottle)

Extra flour

Nonstick baking sheet

MAKES ENOUGH FOR 4 PIZZAS

IF YOU'RE USING A FOOD PROCESSOR:

1. In a bowl, use a whisk to combine the water and yeast until the yeast dissolves. Let it sit for about 15 minutes. It will begin to look foamy.

2. In the food processor, combine the flour and salt using the blade. Add the dissolved yeast and water and pulse until the dough forms a ball and pulls away from the sides of the processor. Be careful not to overmix the dough or it will become gummy and tough.

3. Lightly flour a smooth counter surface. Knead the dough by folding it over itself for about 5 minutes, or until it becomes elastic. Poke it with your finger; when it pops back, it's ready.

4. Spray a large bowl with nonstick spray and place the dough inside. Drape a damp towel over the bowl to keep the dough covered. Let the bowl sit in a warm place for about 45 minutes, or until the dough has doubled in volume.

5. Divide the dough into four equal portions. Form each portion into a ball. (If freezing any of the dough, do so now: wrap it tightly in plastic and store it in a freezer-safe bag.) Spray a bowl with cooking spray and put the dough in the bowl. Cover the bowl with a damp towel and let it sit in a warm place for 20 minutes.

6. Flatten each ball of dough and roll into a thin circle, about ⅛" to ¼" thick. (It should end up being roughly 12" in diameter.) Dust it with flour if it is too sticky.

Pizza Dough (cont'd)

IF YOU'RE MAKING DOUGH BY HAND:

1. In a bowl, use a whisk to combine the water and yeast until the yeast dissolves. Let it sit for about 15 minutes. It will begin to look foamy.

2. Add in flour and salt and stir with a wooden spoon. When the mixture becomes stiff, turn out onto a lightly floured, smooth counter surface and use your hands to knead the dough together. Knead by folding the dough over itself for about 10 minutes or until it becomes elastic. Poke it with your finger; when it pops back, it's ready.

3. Continue with step 4 of food processor directions.

TO FINISH:

1. If you're working with frozen dough, take it out of the freezer a few hours early to let it thaw.

2. Heat the oven to 500°F. If you want a crisper crust, pre-heat the baking sheet in the oven as well.

3. Top the pizza with desired toppings and bake until the crust is golden and the cheese is melted, about 7 to 10 minutes.

QUICKIES

- *Wrap tightly in plastic and freeze what you don't need.*
- *Active dry yeast is found on the baking aisle of your grocery store. It comes in small paper packets, usually in sets of three. Double-check the expiration date before you buy.*
- *Add leftover chopped herbs, olives, or sun-dried tomatoes to make a gourmet-style dough. Just add them when you're kneading the dough.*

Pizza with Basic Tomato Sauce, Mozzarella, and Fresh Basil

FOR SAUCE:

½ tablespoon extra-virgin olive oil

¼ small onion, diced

1 clove garlic, minced (or use a garlic press)

¼ bunch roughly chopped fresh basil (leaves only, no stems)

½ (14-ounce) can crushed tomatoes

Salt and pepper to taste

COOKING ACCESSORIES

Chef's knife

Garlic press (optional)

2-Quart pot

Wooden spoon or
heat-resistant spatula

Nonstick baking sheet

MAKES 1 CUP

1. Heat a saucepan over medium heat and add the olive oil.

2. When the pan is hot, add the onion and cook about 4 minutes, or until soft and translucent but not browned.

3. Add the garlic and cook about 1 minute.

4. Add the basil and tomatoes. Bring to a boil, then reduce the heat to low, cover, and simmer 15 to 30 minutes, stirring occasionally.

5. Season sauce with salt and pepper.

TO ASSEMBLE PIZZA:

1. If you're working with frozen dough, take it out of the freezer a few hours early to let it thaw.

2. Heat the oven to 500°F. If you want a crisper crust, preheat the baking sheet in the oven as well.

3. Flatten one ball of dough and roll into a thin circle, about ⅛" to ¼" thick. (It should end up being roughly 12" in diameter.) Dust it with flour if it is too sticky.

4. Top the pizza with a thin layer of tomato sauce and sprinkle cheese evenly on top. Bake it on a baking sheet until the crust is golden and the cheese is melted, about 7 to 10 minutes.

5. Remove the pizza from the oven and sprinkle basil on top.

QUICKIE

● *Instead of making your own pizza dough, try easy alternatives like pita bread, French bread, lavosh, premade pizza dough, or refrigerated dough you can bake at home.*

FOR PIZZA:

1 recipe Pizza Dough (page 180) (freeze extra dough)

¼ to ½ Basic Tomato Sauce recipe, about ¼ to ½ cup (whole recipe precedes)

¾ cup part-skim shredded mozzarella, or 5 slices fresh mozzarella

3 to 5 fresh basil leaves, roughly chopped

Pizza with Caramelized Onions, Mushroom Ragout, and Fontina Cheese

MUSHROOM RAGOUT:

½ tablespoon butter or extra-virgin olive oil

3 cups assorted mushrooms (e.g., button, portobello, shiitake), sliced into ¼" pieces

1 shallot, chopped

Salt and pepper to taste

1 clove garlic, chopped (or use a garlic press)

2 tablespoons white wine (or sherry or Madeira)

1 teaspoon chopped fresh thyme (leaves only, no stems)

COOKING ACCESSORIES

Chef's knife

10" Skillet

Wooden spoon or heat-resistant spatula

Nonstick baking sheet

1. Melt the butter or pour the olive oil in a large sauté pan over medium high heat.

2. When the pan is hot, add the mushrooms, shallots, salt, and pepper and sauté for about 5 minutes, or until the mushrooms begin to soften and most of the moisture that comes out of the mushrooms evaporates.

3. Add the garlic and cook until fragrant (only 10 seconds or so).

4. Add the wine and scrape up any browned bits from the bottom of the pan. Let the wine cook down and evaporate until the pan is almost dry. Stir in the thyme.

QUICKIES

● *A little planning ahead makes this recipe extremely quick. If you already have extra caramelized onions and mushroom ragout (maybe from last night's Caramelized Onion Frittata with Parmesan and Balsamic Glaze, or Angel Hair with Mushroom Ragout), this pizza can be made in minutes.*

● *Choose your favorite mushrooms for this. Most markets these days have a large variety of both wild and cultivated mushrooms. Wild mushrooms include chantarelle, shiitake, oyster, and porcini. Cultivated includes white button, crimini (which are baby portobellos), and portobellos.*

Pizza with Caramelized Onions (cont'd)

TO PREPARE ONIONS:

1. Heat the oil in a sauté pan over medium low heat.

2. When the pan is heated, add the onions, salt, and pepper. Cook slowly until the onions are very soft and a deep brown, stirring occasionally. This can take about 30 minutes. If you cook them too fast, the outsides will burn before the inside has a chance to cook. The longer the onions cook, the more flavor will develop.

3. Add the vinegar and cook until it evaporates.

CARAMELIZED ONIONS:

1 teaspoon extra-virgin olive oil

1 onion (look for sweet onions like Vidalia or Maui, but any onion will do), sliced into ⅛" slices

Salt and pepper to taste

½ tablespoon balsamic vinegar

TO ASSEMBLE PIZZA:

1. Heat the oven to 500°F. If you want a crisper crust, pre-heat the baking sheet in the oven as well.

2. Top the pizza with the caramelized onions, mushroom ragout, and cheese. Bake it on a baking sheet until the crust is golden and the cheese is melted, about 7 to 10 minutes.

PIZZA:

1 recipe Pizza Dough (page 180) (freeze extra dough)

½ recipe Caramelized Onions (whole recipe precedes)

½ recipe Mushroom Ragout (whole recipe precedes)

½ cup shredded fontina cheese

Pizza with Pesto, Grilled Zucchini, Prosciutto, and Goat Cheese

NUTRIENTS
Antioxidants
Calcium
Folate

YELLOW SQUASH AND ZUCCHINI:

1 small yellow squash

1 small zucchini

1 teaspoon extra-virgin olive oil

Salt and pepper to taste

Drizzle of balsamic vinegar

1 tablespoon chopped fresh basil leaves

1. Heat the barbecue or grill pan on medium high heat.

2. Trim the ends of the squash; slice the squash lengthwise into ¼" strips.

3. Brush each side of the squash with olive oil and sprinkle with salt and pepper.

4. Grill until there are good grill marks on the squash (the black lines left from the grill), about 2 minutes.

5. Flip the squash with tongs and finish cooking until crisp-tender. Remove the squash from the grill.

6. Brush the squash with a thin layer of the balsamic vinegar and sprinkle with the basil.

COOKING ACCESSORIES

Chef's knife

Garlic press (optional)

Food processor

Grill pan

Brush

Tongs

Nonstick baking sheet

TO PREPARE PESTO:

Combine all the ingredients in a food processor or blender and blend until smooth.

TO ASSEMBLE PIZZA:

1. Heat the oven to 500°F. If you want a crisper crust, preheat the baking sheet in the oven as well.

2. Spread the pesto on the dough, then top the pizza with the grilled squash, prosciutto, and goat cheese and bake it on a baking sheet until the crust is golden and the cheese is melted, about 7 to 10 minutes.

QUICKIE

- *To save money and temptation, buy only the amount of prosciutto that you need. Most deli counters sell it by the slice, so you don't need an entire package.*

PESTO:

1 cup fresh basil leaves, packed

1 tablespoon pine nuts, toasted

2 tablespoons grated Parmesan cheese

1 clove garlic, chopped (or use a garlic press)

2 tablespoons extra-virgin olive oil

Juice of half a lemon

Salt and pepper to taste

PIZZA:

1 recipe Pizza Dough (page 180) (freeze extra dough)

½ recipe Caramelized Onions (whole recipe precedes)

½ recipe Mushroom Ragout (whole recipe precedes)

½ cup shredded fontina cheese

Pizza with Shaved Fennel, Shallots, Green Olives, and Mozzarella

NUTRIENTS
Antioxidants
Calcium
Folate

1 recipe Pizza Dough (page 180) (freeze extra dough)

¼ cup fennel, shaved as thin as possible with a knife

1 shallot, cut in thin slices

1 tablespoon roughly chopped pitted green olives

Salt to taste

¾ cup part-skim shredded mozzarella or 5 slices fresh mozzarella

Crushed red chili flakes (optional)

COOKING ACCESSORIES
Chef's knife
Nonstick baking sheet

1. Heat the oven to 450°F. If you want a crisper crust, preheat the baking sheet in the oven as well.

2. Top the pizza dough with the fennel, shallot, olives, salt, mozzarella, and chili flakes (if using) and bake it on a baking sheet until the crust is golden and the cheese is melted, about 7 to 10 minutes.

QUICKIES

- *Use your favorite veggies on this as long as you slice them all very thin. For example, zucchini, mushrooms, and eggplant would taste great and be an easy way to get rid of extra veggies you have in your fridge.*

- *Shallots are similar to onions but have a more delicate, sweeter flavor. You can find them in your grocery store next to onions, or sometimes near the garlic. They're perfect for meals-for-one because they are much smaller than onions.*

- *Fennel is a bulb that is found in the produce section, usually near other root veggies and cabbages. It has long green stalks and a white base. At the top of the stalks are the "fronds," which can be used as a garnish. It has a slight licorice flavor and can be used raw or cooked.*

Pizza with Turkey Italian Sausage, Ricotta Cheese, and Fresh Basil

1. Heat the oven to 450°F. If you want a crisper crust, pre-heat the baking sheet in the oven as well.

2. Combine the ricotta, garlic, and salt and stir well.

3. Spread the ricotta mixture onto the pizza dough. Top the pizza with the sliced sausage and bake it on a baking sheet until the crust is golden and the cheese is melted, about 7 to 10 minutes.

4. Remove the pizza from the oven and sprinkle basil on top.

QUICKIE

● *For a more cheesy texture on this pizza, substitute half of the ricotta with part-skim shredded mozzarella.*

NUTRIENTS
Antioxidants
Calcium
Folate

1 recipe Pizza Dough (page 180) (freeze extra dough)

½ cup low-fat or nonfat ricotta cheese

1 small clove garlic, minced (or use a garlic press)

Salt to taste

1 link turkey Italian sausage, sliced into ¼" slices

3 to 5 fresh basil leaves, roughly chopped

COOKING ACCESSORIES
Chef's knife

Garlic press (optional)

Nonstick baking sheet

Jim Davis

"Vegetables are a must on a diet.
I suggest carrot cake, zucchini
bread, and pumpkin pie."

CHAPTER EIGHT

desserts

sweets for my sweet, sugar for my honey

It almost seems as if we could chart our lives by which artificial sweetener we substituted for sugar. For those of you who still have flashbacks of your mothers drinking Tab like it was going out of Twiggy-style, welcome to our world.

Talk about a bad flashback. Almost makes you wonder what kind of "trip" your mother was on in the late 1970s given her propensity to throw back all of those Tabs. Then there were all those years of high school and college when, instead of carrying around a Nalgene bottle full of artesian-filtered natural spring water, you sported a red wax-paper cup from the cafeteria for Diet Coke consumption. And, if your calculations are correct, you consumed about 160 ounces of Diet Coke a day for a solid six years of your life; that's 350,400 ounces of Diet Coke from ages sixteen to twenty-two. That's a problem. Although perhaps not for the shareholders of Coca Cola, Inc. After graduation you tried to kick the habit, but at times you thought that quitting your Rabbit might be an easier task. Finally, after years of considering inventing "The Diet Coke Patch," your consuming habits have waned, only to be replaced by wine. (We'll explore the ramifications of that little "issue" later in Chapter 9, so hold tight—you're not off the hook just yet.)

Now, almost thirty years after your first artificial-sweetener memory, the same woman whose Tab fad kick-started your craving, your mother, is the one barking at you each time you empty a packet of sweetener into your coffee or imbibe a Diet Coke, claiming, "You're going to get cancer if you keep using that *stuff*." You dismissively roll your eyes and explain to her that the odds of you getting cancer from artificial sweeteners are about as likely as you winning the lottery. Ironically enough, each time you drive by the sign that says "Lotto up to $35 Million," you honestly think, "I bet I could win." Freaky. Then you start to rethink that ache on your left calf. Could be cancer. Or that freckle on your right arm. Again, cancer. After you have called every single one of your friends who are in their first-year medical rotations and they (all seven of them) have reassured you that you don't have cancer, you start to become a wee bit more rational. Still, however, you wonder.

What is Splenda? This artificial sweetener is made of sucralose, which is made from sugar that is chemically combined with chlorine. Now you're pretty sure that ingesting chlorine isn't the hottest idea, considering it turned your hair green by the end of each summer. Splenda selectively replaces three hydrogen-oxygen groups on the sugar molecule with three chlorine atoms. Then poof!—sucralose is born! Now, don't lose it; what you didn't know is that chlorine is naturally found in a variety of foods, like salt. (Remember, the Cl part of NaCl?)

The characteristics of sucralose make it impossible for our bodies to break it down for energy, thus it does not contribute a significant amount of calories as it passes through. And because we know that you're still reeling over that freckle on your right arm, put your mind at ease: Splenda appears to be safe and is not suspected to cause cancer. Therefore, if you are trying to watch your weight, Splenda can be a good alternative to sugar though it's probably best not to make it a staple of your diet. (Remember, 1 teaspoon sugar has only 16 calories.) And, unlike most artificial sweeteners, Splenda can also be used measure-for-measure in baking, which is why you see many sugar-free or low-calorie baked goods containing it.

Now what about those other artificial sweeteners? In 1996, the FDA approved aspartame for use in all foods and beverages. Aspartame, also known as Equal and NutraSweet, has been approved in 100 other nations and has not been shown to cause cancer. Though artificial sweeteners have not been associated with adverse health risks, some individuals claim that aspartame gives them headaches. The FDA has received complaints about possible side effects from aspartame, but investigations by the Centers for Disease Control and Prevention didn't link those effects to aspartame. Clearly, despite claims that they appear to be unrelated to aspartame, this is a controversial topic.

Unlike aspartame, saccharin had been shown to cause certain types of cancer in rats; for this reason, the FDA proposed a ban on saccharin—more commonly known as Sweet'N Low—in 1977 and required foods containing saccharin to carry a warning label that the product could be hazardous to your health. After further studies from the FDA and National Cancer Institute failed to link saccharin to any form of cancer in humans, the warning requirement was removed in 2000. The topic is still controversial among many. Rats, rats, rats!

Now that you are utterly confused and lamenting over the freckle on your arm again, you're still left with the question: What should you use? You are always best using the natural product—sugar. Just remember, to use it in moderation. Although many appear safe today, artificial sweeteners are being consumed in higher quantities than ever before; it's too soon to know what the long-term ramifications will be. So once again, perhaps we should just chalk it up to inevitability and listen to our moms.

Baked Peaches Stuffed with Amaretti Cookies

NUTRIENTS
Antioxidants

½ ripe peach, pit removed

2 amaretti cookies, crushed

1 teaspoon peach brandy (regular brandy will do)

1 teaspoon Splenda

⅛ teaspoon cinnamon

¼ teaspoon vanilla extract

1 teaspoon margarine

COOKING ACCESSORIES

Chef's knife

Small oven-safe dish, e.g., 9" × 5" loaf pan

1. Heat the oven to 350°F.

2. Combine the cookies, brandy, Splenda, cinnamon, vanilla, and margarine and mix well. Mound the amaretti filling into the peach half.

3. Set the peach inside a small oven-safe dish. Bake it for about 30 minutes, then cover with foil and bake for another 15 minutes, or until the peach is tender. This can be served hot or cold. Try it with a scoop of low-fat ice cream.

QUICKIES

- *Amaretti cookies are Italian almond-flavored cookies. They have a delicious flavor that goes very well with peaches, but you could always substitute your favorite cookie instead. Oatmeal, chocolate chip, or snickerdoodles would all be great.*

- *To remove the pit from a peach, start at the stem end and run a knife around the whole fruit, cutting all the way down to the pit. Gently twist the two halves apart and the pit can be popped out. If it doesn't easily come out, carefully cut around it with the tip of a paring knife.*

Baked Stuffed Banana with Graham Cracker Spoons

1. Heat the oven to 350°F.

2. Tear off a piece of foil that is large enough to wrap around the banana. Spray the foil with cooking spray. Leaving the skin on, slice the banana lengthwise but don't cut all the way through so that it separates into two halves. Carefully open it a little to make room for the filling. Fill the opening with the hazelnut spread and marshmallows. Cover tightly with the foil in case any of the chocolate oozes out.

3. Place the banana on a baking sheet and bake it for about 20 minutes or until the banana is tender.

4. Unwrap the banana and slightly pull the slit open. (Be careful of the escaping steam.) Use the graham crackers to scoop out the banana and filling.

QUICKIE

- *This can also just as easily be done on the grill. You'll get lots of "ooohs" and "aaahs" from your guests.*

NUTRIENTS
Antioxidants
Calcium
Fiber

1 ripe banana

Cooking spray

1 to 2 tablespoons chocolate hazelnut spread, such as Nutella

2 tablespoon mini marshmallows

1 whole graham cracker (the whole rectangle)

COOKING ACCESSORIES
Chef's knife or paring knife
Aluminum foil

Caramel Apple Strudel

NUTRIENTS
Antioxidants
Fiber
Folate
Low-fat

2 Braeburn or Gala apples, peeled, cored and cut into ¼" wedges

2 tablespoons Splenda

¼ teaspoon cinnamon

⅛ teaspoon nutmeg

½ teaspoon vanilla extract

⅛ teaspoon ground ginger

Nonstick cooking spray

5 sheets frozen phyllo dough, thawed according to instructions

Butter spray, such as I Can't Believe It's Not Butter Spray

6 chewy caramel candies, unwrapped

4 tablespoons whipped topping

COOKING ACCESSORIES
Chef's knife

Bowl

Nonstick baking sheet

MAKES 4 SERVINGS

1. Heat the oven to 400°F.

2. In a bowl, combine the apples, Splenda, cinnamon, nutmeg, vanilla, and ginger.

3. Spray a baking sheet with the nonstick spray. Carefully place one sheet of phyllo on the baking sheet and spray evenly with the butter spray. Place the next layer of phyllo on top and spray with the butter spray. Continue until all five sheets of phyllo are used and each layer is sprayed with butter.

4. Evenly distribute the apple mixture at one end of the phyllo. Top the apple mixture with the caramel candies and tightly roll up the phyllo to form a log.

5. Fold up the edges of the log so that no juices leak out during baking. Position the log on the baking sheet and spray it with the butter spray. With a sharp knife, cut three slits in the top so that steam can escape while it's baking.

6. Bake about 20 minutes, or until the phyllo is golden brown. Remove the strudel from the oven. Cool the strudel slightly, slice it into servings, and top it with whipped topping.

QUICKIE

- *Phyllo dough (also spelled filo) is in the freezer section of your grocery store near frozen pie crusts and other desserts. It is paper-thin layers of dough that create a light and flaky texture once baked. Phyllo dries out very quickly. To keep it from cracking, lay the sheets out flat and loosely cover them with a damp dish towel—if it's dripping wet the dough will get too soggy.*

Chocolate Fondue with Seasonal Fruits

1. Place the chocolate in a microwave-safe bowl and cook it in 30-second intervals until the chocolate is fully melted, stirring between intervals.

2. Slice the fruits into bite-sized pieces and dip them into your melted chocolate. If the chocolate starts to cool and harden, just pop it back into the micro until it's melted again.

QUICKIE

● *If you're not sure what fruits are in season, it's usually whichever ones are cheapest at the grocery store, since they're readily available. Some seasonal favorites: Spring: strawberries, blueberries; Summer: peaches, plums; Fall: honeydew, apples; Winter: kiwi, bananas.*

NUTRIENTS
Antioxidants
Fiber

2 to 3 ounces of your favorite chocolate (If it's not chips, just roughly chop it.)

Your choice of seasonal fruits, about 1 handful total. If using things like apples or bananas, you'll need 3 or 4 slices of each.

COOKING ACCESSORIES

Microwave-safe bowl (look on the bottom of the bowl, where it's usually specified)

Chef's knife

Cranberry-Orange Bread Pudding

NUTRIENTS
Antioxidants
Calcium
Low-fat

¼ cup dried cranberries

2 tablespoons orange liqueur, such as Cointreau

1 cup fat-free milk

1 teaspoon vanilla extract

2 eggs, lightly beaten with a fork

¼ teaspoon cinnamon

Pinch of nutmeg

¼ cup Splenda

Zest of 1 orange

3 cups Hawaiian sweet bread, cut into 1" cubes (Portuguese sweet bread or challah bread are great substitutes)

Cooking spray

COOKING ACCESSORIES
Small mixing bowl

Microplane

Chef's knife or bread knife

Large mixing bowl

9" × 5" Loaf pan

Aluminum foil

MAKES 4 TO 5 SERVINGS

1. Combine the cranberries and orange liqueur in a small bowl and set aside.

2. Combine the milk, vanilla, eggs, cinnamon, nutmeg, Splenda, and orange zest in a large bowl. Mix well. Add the bread and the cranberry/liqueur mixture.

3. Spray a loaf pan with nonstick spray. Pour the mixture into the pan and let it soak, covered with foil, in the refrigerator for 1 hour.

4. Heat the oven to 350°F.

5. Bake the pudding for 30 minutes, then uncover it and bake 10 more minutes or until a knife inserted into the center comes out clean. Serve!

QUICKIES

● *This versatile and delicious dessert can be served hot or cold.*

● *Bread pudding freezes really well once it has been baked. In order to help portion control, go ahead and separate this into individual servings, wrap tightly, and freeze. That way you can have a homemade dessert without too much guilt.*

● *Hawaiian Sweet Bread (usually under the brand name "King's") is a soft, delicate bread with a subtle sweetness. You can find it in any grocery store either in the bread aisle or with the freshly baked bread.*

Gingersnap and Pumpkin Parfait

1. In a small bowl, combine the pumpkin purée, pumpkin pie spice, and Splenda.

2. Place half of the crushed gingersnaps in a tall glass, such as a martini glass.

3. Cover the gingersnaps with half of the pudding, then half of the pumpkin mixture. Continue layering with remaining gingersnaps, then pudding, then pumpkin. Top dessert with the whipped topping.

QUICKIE

● *This is a great holiday-time alternative to the traditional pies, which contain much more fat and calories.*

NUTRIENTS
Antioxidants
Calcium
Fiber
Low-fat

¼ cup canned pumpkin purée

¼ teaspoon pumpkin pie spice

1 tablespoon Splenda

¼ cup crushed gingersnap cookies (small pieces, not crumbs)

½ cup nonfat vanilla pudding, prepared according to package instructions (look for pudding with calcium)

1 tablespoon nonfat whipped topping

COOKING ACCESSORIES

Whisk or electric hand mixer

Martini glass, optional for more dramatic presentation

Grilled Pineapple with Vanilla-Coconut Ricotta

½ teaspoon vegetable oil

¼ cup nonfat ricotta cheese

Zest of half a lime

¼ teaspoon vanilla extract

1 teaspoon Splenda

1 teaspoon non-fat milk

2 slices fresh pineapple, cut ½" thick

2 tablespoons shredded sweetened coconut, toasted until light
golden brown

COOKING ACCESSORIES

Brush

Chef's knife

Microplane

Bowl

Grill or grill pan

Tongs

1. Heat the grill or grill pan on high heat and brush with the oil.

2. Combine the ricotta, lime zest, vanilla, Splenda, and milk.

3. Grill the pineapple slices for about 4 minutes per side, or until they have caramelized on the outside but have not become too mushy.

4. Remove the pineapple to a plate and top it with ricotta mixture. Sprinkle with the toasted coconut.

QUICKIES

● *To cut a whole pineapple, first cut off the top and bottom so it sits flat on your cutting board. Then run the knife down from top to bottom, peeling off the skin. To slice, turn it on its side and cut it into rounds. (Coring it is not necessary.)*

● *You'll have to buy more pineapple than you need, so freeze the extra and use it in a smoothie with vanilla yogurt, banana, and strawberries. Or eat it on its own . . . with a chilled Sauvignon Blanc.*

● *You can toast coconut in a dry pan (without oil) on the stove over medium low heat, stirring occasionally, until it's lightly golden brown. You can also put the coconut on a sheet tray and toast it in a 350°F oven or toaster oven for about 5 minutes.*

Plum and Peach Shortcake with Cinnamon Cream

1. Combine the plum, peach, Splenda, and brandy. Let them sit for 20 minutes, or until some of the juices from the fruits come out.

2. In a separate bowl, combine the yogurt and cinnamon.

3. Spoon the fruit mixture on top of the angel food cake, then drizzle cinnamon cream on top.

QUICKIE

- *This would also be great with pound cake instead of angel food cake.*

NUTRIENTS
Antioxidants
Calcium
Fiber
Low-fat*
•*Low-fat only if angel food cake is used*

½ small ripe plum, cut into thin wedges

¼ ripe peach, cut into thin wedges

1 teaspoon Splenda

½ teaspoon peach brandy (regular brandy will work, too)

2 tablespoons nonfat vanilla yogurt

¼ teaspoon cinnamon

1 slice store-bought angel food cake (freeze extra cake) or pound cake

COOKING ACCESSORIES

Chef's knife

2 bowls

Rustic Summer Berry Tart

NUTRIENTS
Antioxidants
Fiber
Low-fat

1 sheet frozen puff pastry, thawed
    according to package
    instructions

1 cup quartered strawberries, stems
    removed

½ cup blueberries, picked over for
    mushy or rotten berries

1 cup raspberries, picked over for
    mushy or rotten berries

½ cup blackberries, picked over for
    mushy or rotten berries

1 teaspoon vanilla extract

2 to 3 tablespoons Splenda,
    depending on how sweet the
    berries are (taste some first)

Zest of 1 lemon

COOKING ACCESSORIES

Chef's knife

Microplane

Nonstick baking sheet

MAKES 6 SERVINGS

1. Heat the oven to 350°F.

2. Spray a baking sheet with cooking spray. Lay the sheet of thawed pastry onto the sheet.

3. Combine the berries, vanilla, half of the Splenda, and lemon zest in a bowl. Mound the fruit mixture onto the center of the pastry and fold the edges over to form a circle, overlapping the dough as necessary. Sprinkle the tart with remaining Splenda.

4. Bake the tart for 30 minutes, or until the crust is golden.

QUICKIES

- *Use individual pie tins to cut the recipe down; the baking time would remain about the same.*

- *This is great to serve at a dinner party because it has a handmade look to it, as if you slaved away for hours.*

- *Puff pastry is found in the freezer section of your grocery store, usually in the specialty or dessert sections. You'll need to let it thaw enough so that it doesn't crack when you work with it. The process of making puff pastry is time consuming and tedious, so take advantage of this ready-made, great product!*

- *The easiest way to zest a lemon is to use a microplane. Just be careful to remove only the yellow part of the skin because the white pith is very bitter. If you don't have a microplane, you can peel the skin off using a vegetable peeler and finely chop it with a knife.*

Vanilla Bean Frozen Yogurt with Figs, Honey, and Pistachios

1. Scoop the frozen yogurt into a bowl and top it with the figs.

2. Drizzle honey all over the figs and scatter the nuts on top.

QUICKIES

- *Look for frozen yogurt with calcium. It can be a great way to get some extra calcium in for the day.*

- *The most common type of fig is the Black Mission Fig. It has a deep purple skin and is oval in shape. Dried figs are a delicious snack and are packed full of iron and calcium.*

- *Toast nuts on a baking sheet in a 300°F oven for just a few minutes. They are done cooking as soon as you can smell them. Overcooking them will burn their oils and they'll become bitter. You can also toast them in a dry pan (without oil) on the stove; toss them occasionally.*

NUTRIENTS
Antioxidants
Calcium
Fiber

1 scoop low-fat vanilla bean frozen yogurt

2 small figs, stems trimmed, cut into quarters

1 tablespoon lavender honey (or your favorite variety)

1 tablespoon roughly chopped toasted pistachios

COOKING ACCESSORIES
Ice cream scoop

Chef's knife

Dean Martin

"You're not drunk if you can lie
on the floor without holding on."

CHAPTER NINE

beverages
going down, nice and smooth

In our estimation, there are only two types of beverages: alcoholic and non-alcoholic. And while our preference of the two might sway given the difficulty of our day at work or how many times we had to remind ourselves that yes, in order to fit into the latest bridesmaid dress, we were going to have to exercise, we don't have a beverage of choice.

While beverages might seem like the redheaded stepchild to food, their nutritional benefits are equally as important, if not more so. From water, to wine, to milk, you'll be surprised just how crucial beverages are to your health. Remember: There is a way to have your vodka and drink it too.

Imbibing: Your Tall Drink of Water

While admitting that we have a "type" of guy might limit our dating odds with gentlemen in other walks of life, we'll take our chances. You might have a thing for the shy bookworm who reconfigures his computer motherboard on Friday nights; or perhaps the wiseass, Ivy League, suited investment banker is your weakness; or maybe you're insane over the intense, type-A attorney who color-codes his Post-its, highlighters, and number-two pencils. Whichever it is, there's one thing we know: Whoever does it for us in adulthood is not the same guy who threw us into complete lovesick chaos in adolescence.

Consider the brief period of time when crushes were concentrated to a specific athletic persuasion: If your former flames are anything like ours, then they've most likely been reduced to a bunch of fat, balding, narcissistic oafs whom you would immediately red-shirt for the love season of today. And until you find your tall drink of water, trust us on this one: You won't find him on any team rosters from yesteryear. Whether you discover him at the next company outing or under another serendipitous circumstance, we're confident you'll find your sleeper (and your keeper). But until then, you'll need to quench your thirst with something else.

Filling the void with substances like wine, beer, cocktails, coffee, or Diet Coke (in no particular order) is *not* the answer. In the spirit of replacing your usual love-quests with men who will enhance your well-being and livelihood, we would recommend the same for beverage consumption. We're fairly certain you're not completely satisfied, but by replacing your current liquid lineup with *water*, however, you will find satisfaction. Water makes up about 60 to 70 percent of our body composition and is critical to maintaining health. It is at the crux of nutrition and aids in a variety of bodily functions:

- Transportation of nutrients
- Transportation of waste and excretion (helps remove them from the body)
- Digestion and absorption of proteins, carbohydrates, and water-soluble vitamins (necessary to deliver nutrients to cells of the body)

- Maintenance of body temperature (essential to make sure enzymes, hormones, and all other aspects of the body are functioning)
- Lubrication of joints (allows for movement of arms, legs, etc. without pain)
- Protection of organs (cushions and protects from damage, including absorbing shocks)
- Prevention of constipation (enough said . . .)

Given the above, it's no wonder we can live significantly longer without food than without water. Although everyone needs different amounts of water for optimum hydration, most of us should drink eight 8-ounce glasses a day. Consider the benefits of "getting enough":

Waiting to drink water until you are thirsty is too late. Waiting until your twentieth high school reunion to find your first husband might be too late.

Thirst is a sign that you are already dehydrated. The lack of a raging libido is a sign that you've waited too long to have sex.

Drinking water throughout the day prevents dehydration. Having passionate, intimate, satisfying sex on a regular basis reduces your risk of being a sullen bitch.

Dehydration can be caused by many different factors such as illness, alcohol consumption, high temperature and/or high humidity, high salt intake, exercise, age, caffeine consumption, medications, traveling on an airplane, or high protein intake. Lack of sexual intimacy can be caused by many different factors such as men (or lack thereof), alcohol consumption (or lack thereof), propensity to stress (about lack of sex), exercise (lack thereof and consequently feeling like a beluga whale), age (of all men, whether they are too young or too old), medications (valium, antianxieties, antidepressants, etc.), and travel (or lack thereof).

Thirst is also often confused with hunger. If you are thirsty, it is very possible that you think you are hungry. Therefore, it's always a good idea to drink water before eating to determine whether you're actually hungry. Lack of sex can be confused with being depressed. If you are depressed, it is very possible that you are deprived of having satisfying sex. Therefore, it's always a good idea to have sex before seeing a therapist.

Although it is not scientific fact, it is believed that drinking eight glasses of water per day can boost your metabolism. Having sex eight times a day will boost your ego.

Switching your sweetened iced tea, gourmet coffee drinks, juices, sports drinks, and sodas to water will definitely help you lose weight, since you'll be cutting out a lot of calories. Switching your current loser male companion (or lack of male companion) to exercise, a balanced and healthy diet, decreased stress, a good therapist, and being in love with a wonderful, thoughtful, hilarious, and loving boyfriend (or a fabulous vibrator) will also help you lose weight.

All Shapes and Sizes (and Flavors!)

There are many varieties of water. Whether you drink tap water, bottled water, club soda, seltzer, or sparkling water, the benefits are the same. (A penis is a penis is a penis.) Be aware that some flavored waters contain calories, which regular water does not. Always read the food label to find out. *Also note that tonic is not water—it is soda.* If you are prone to bloating, beware: Carbonated water can lead to increased bloating. Conversely, flat water can help decrease the bloating caused by high salt intake by flushing out some of the fluids your body is retaining.

Keep in mind that you do get some water from non-water sources. Some beverages and certain foods, particularly fruits and vegetables, contribute to your daily water intake. While the water you get from fruits and vegetables is very

important, you should still aim for eight glasses of actual water a day. Another caveat: Caffeinated beverages such as coffee and tea are diuretics, which make you need to urinate. So, although you do get some fluid from these morning beverage necessities, they will cause you to *lose* fluids.

Just when you thought you couldn't handle another nutritional recommendation, here's our last one (in this chapter): *Always keep a glass or water bottle with you—on your desk, in your car, on the train, or in your purse.* Much like a booty call at your disposal lets you maintain your libido, keeping a bottle or glass of water near you at all times will let you maintain hydration.

Boozehounds, Bratwursts, and Beers: The Truth Behind Conspicuous Alcohol Consumption

Many of us take periodic trips down memory lane by rummaging through the thirty-five photo albums we so carefully crafted during our collegiate stint. In the midst of the overwhelming nostalgia, you're taken aback by the fabulous design and originality of said albums. (C'mon, who hasn't spent eight hours organizing slobbering drunk pictures of herself and her fifty-seven friends from college?) Suddenly you realize you should apply this rediscovered skill to the project you've been avoiding at work . . . though we'll readily admit those albums are more engaging than marketing collateral design and the company database.

We wouldn't be surprised if, while reminiscing, you had a few mini-breakdowns as you realized your carefree days of college—sleeping until noon, hitting the hay at 3 A.M. (on sober nights), rolling to the nearest campus pub for a few pitchers of Miller High Life on a casual Tuesday afternoon, and navigating your schedule around classes that began after 11 A.M.—are *over*. Likewise, if your reactions were similar to ours, you found yourself gawking at the *three* chins you didn't realize you had grown during campus life. Flipping through each page with growing concern, you speed-dial your best friend and ream her for convincing you that you looked stunning in that royal blue strapless dress. We've all borrowed *that dress*. The one owned by a budding beauty queen down the hall who claimed to have won *Miss Peanut Queen Georgia 1995*. On this particular occasion, your charming escort was a hot soccer player. You remember thinking that after he took one look at you, he was overcome by your beauty and wanted to sire your children. And yes, you openly admit that after you'd thrown

back two preparty cocktails you had already decided upon all three of your unborn children's names (first and middle). You examine the picture more carefully and realize you actually resemble a blue-foiled bratwurst displayed at the Piggly Wiggly. You should have doused yourself in Scent of Sauerkraut instead of Coco Chanel. You knew you had put on weight in college, but only now do you realize you weren't just a little plump; you were indeed *fat*.

What's strange is that in the years since your blue bratwurst dress days, you have slimmed down, or at least you think you have. Perhaps it's because the ritual late-night nosh has now become a once- or twice-a-week phenomenon and not a nightly occurrence. Or perhaps it's because instead of single-handedly polishing off a pitcher and half of beer during a broomball game, you now try to keep it classy with your colleagues by polishing off bottles of wine.

Comforted by the fact that you no longer have *that* many friends who own a kegerator, you are still occasionally concerned by your mother continuously warning you that "alcoholism runs in the family." But you have to wonder, whose family doesn't alcoholism run in? Then it becomes a moot point, because if you are an alcoholic, then so are all of your friends. You decide that if you were ever rounded up like a herd of intoxicated cattle, you'd get the group discount rate at Betty Ford. It would almost be like going to Canyon Ranch or Club Med, only the vacation would last for twenty-eight days. Your visions of a relaxing spa-esque rehab vanish when you have your annual checkup and your doctor asks, "Approximately how many drinks do you have a week?"

Confident that your days of ridiculous consumption are now only legendary, you might shrug your shoulders and honestly answer, "Somewhere between ten to twenty, on average." You've mentally calculated that you consume approximately one to two glasses of wine on weeknights and, depending on the weekend and whose birthday you're celebrating, the number increases. Your doctor calmly puts down her stethoscope, looks you dead in the eye, and says, "That's unacceptable." Suddenly you think that your mother has called her ahead of time, and bribed her to read you the riot act about your drinking habits. The lecture continues and you listen closely, searching for any of your mother's catch phrases; none surface, and you are forced to listen. While you insist that drinking red wine is good for you and that women in the South of France are living well into their 100s, her implacably stern face assures you that you've misinterpreted the facts. Completely deflated, you head back to work and call one of your friends to see if she wants to come over for dinner. You do this knowing full well that in order to lift your spirits, after giving her the play-by-play on your recent medical advice, the two of you will polish off a bottle of wine.

Only a few days after your OB-GYN-lifestyles lecture are you ready to admit that one light beer, one glass of wine, or one 4-ounce serving of a hard alcohol is indeed the optimal amount of alcohol consumption for a woman per day. In order to avoid future barrages of "how-to-live-your-life" and still hit the town with joie de vivre, you might consider transcribing these four tips onto laminated flash cards to keep in your purse.

1. More does not always mean better. Everything in *moderation*, as you've heard ad nauseum.
2. Drinking red wine is good for your heart only if you have one drink per day. (It's two per day if you're a man. Once again, we get the raw end of the deal.) Drinking in excess is not good for your heart or any other part of your body—that is, it can lead to serious health problems . . . unless you're a freakish living legend due to the fact that you have four kidneys and two livers.

3. A drink does not equal whatever can fit in a glass—meaning huge pitchers of margaritas do not count as one drink. One drink is equal to 12 ounces of beer, 5 ounces of wine, or 1.5 ounces of 80-proof distilled spirits.

4. Every drink does not have the same number of calories, so choose your drinks wisely. Check out the list of some drinks and the calorie content of each one listed in the chart.

"Here's to Your Waistline" Options

Not that we're encouraging your boozing habit, it's simply that we have sympathy, oh wait, empathy. And to boot, you can now tell your doctor that you are at least attempting to curb your boozing habits to reasonable levels. If you've figured it out, light beer, wine, or distilled spirits with a non-caloric mixer (club soda, diet tonic) are your best bet, calorie-wise. Try these lower-calorie drinks:

- Wine spritzer: white wine with Diet 7-Up or club soda (7 oz.)
- Champagne (5 oz.)
- Vodka and club soda (*not* tonic) (7 oz.)
- Gin and diet tonic (7 oz.)

Cocktails, Cocktails, Cocktails: How Many Are You Consuming?

Beverage	Serving Size	Approx. Calories
Margarita (plain)	8 oz.	500
Piña colada or daiquiri	4.5 oz.	200–250
Rum and Coke	7 oz.	175–200
Martini	3 oz.	160–180
Regular beer	12 oz.	150
Light beer*	12 oz.	100
Red wine*	5 oz.	100
White wine*	5 oz.	100
80-proof distilled spirits (gin, rum, vodka, whiskey), neat or on the rocks	1.5 oz.	100

*Here's to Your Waistline Options

So whether it's wine, water, bourbon, or beer, your imbibing habits are equally as important to your health and nutrition as the other food groups. With that said, read on in Chapter 10 for other delicious cocktails and entrees that won't enable the return of those three chins from college days and won't require door-prize memberships to 24-Hour Fitness for you and your guests.

M.F.K. Fisher

"Sharing food with another human
being is an intimate act that should
not be indulged in lightly."

CHAPTER TEN

let us entertain you
we're very versatile

The last impromptu gathering at your apartment spawned something so horrific, you swore off entertaining for the balance of your single life. While you don't recall all the details, you occasionally have flashbacks resembling a low-budget, made-for-TV movie starring Tara Reid and a handful of her D-list friends.

There was noshing of peanut M&Ms out of Tupperware circa 1984, imbibing of Red Bull and Smirnoff from red plastic cups recycled from college, and grilling of Wonder Bread with Velveeta in a George Foreman that hadn't been cleaned for two weeks. You never imagined the evening would spin into a chaotic entertaining hell. It was as inevitable as avoiding crow's feet (without Botox treatment), however, given that your apartment was the size of a shoe box and your idea of preparing an edible meal was microwaving a Stouffer's frozen dinner and dividing it (equally of course) among your guests. Not cool.

Well, we have news for you. While the *M&Ms in Tupperware* film noir flashbacks may persist, your inability to properly host and entertain was as much a passing phase as your pubescent attitude problem and affinity for big bangs. Moreover, your aversion to playing the ultimate hostess can be rectified by sundry simple entertaining suggestions. Minuscule apartments and archaic hand-me-down dishes can easily be incorporated and tactfully leveraged to create festive gatherings. While you might still be embarrassed by your lack of matching Restoration Hardware furniture and color-coordinated napkin rings, we're confident your culinary aptitude will outshine what you perceive to be your domestic hovel. Daunting as it may be, cooking for four, six, or eight can be just as simple as cooking for one. Impossible, you shrug. You've just begun to master cooking for one. Truth be told, much of your domestic suffering and failure to cook savory meals was based on your lack of experience and confidence. Now that you have both of these things, you should never be ashamed to invite friends over again!

Location, Location, Location

Your mother continuously reminded you, first things first. Entertaining is no exception. Prior to creating a menu and launching into grocery shopping, you'll have to assess your desired location to entertain. Your living situation will most likely dictate your event, which is why we recommend assessing the venue before you finalize the scope of the meal. Each of us has moved upward every year since we graduated from high school, so we know our way around more living spaces across this globe than Oprah's real estate investment advisor (three of us, nearly ten years out of college each . . . well, you do the math). What follows are a few handy tips we've accrued from our basements, studios, apartments, condos, and shared houses. We'll go from smallest to biggest.

studio or small apartment

The postage stamp you call home is your oasis against the mayhem and nonsense. It's your bungalow of love where you seek refuge, and you're ready to share it with your friends. Whether you throw a double-date dinner with another couple, a brunch with your three closest girlfriends, or a fabulously raucous cocktail party with your dearest party animals, you need to consider the following:

Dinner for Four

You're working with a small space and you want your guests to feel comfortable. If you have a kitchen nook that is large enough for a table that seats four, then you're set for dinner. In honor of your little pied-a-terre, cook a meal that enhances its comfort and warmth. This dinner for four could be leveraged as a girls' night to discuss your newest crush whom you spotted at the local watering hole last Friday happy hour or a prescreening of the boy you're dating to ensure he passes the test with your best friend and her boyfriend. *Multiply each recipe and its ingredients by four.*

girls' night menu for four

COCKTAIL Cosmos (obviously . . .); Baja Bob's low-carb Cosmopolitan Mix is amazing! Just add vodka and float a thin slice of orange as garnish.

SALAD Classic Caprese Salad (page 52)

Hot Tip Assemble earlier in the day, cover, and refrigerate until ready to serve.

ENTRÉE Seared Pepperonata Tuna Steak (page 137)

Hot Tip Prepare pepperonata topping the day before, cover, and refrigerate. Reheat in a saucepan or skillet before serving.

SIDE Sautéed Spinach (page 80)

DESSERT Vanilla Bean Frozen Yogurt with Figs, Honey, and Pistachios (page 203)

dinner date menu for four

COCKTAIL Red and white wine

HORS D'OEUVRE Scampi-Style Shrimp (page 138), recipe times three

Hot Tip Serve this as an appetizer. You can make it earlier in the day, cover, and refrigerate. Serve it chilled or at room temperature with toothpicks.

SALAD Iceberg Wedge with Blue Cheese Vinaigrette (page 48).

Hot Tip Make vinaigrette the day before and refrigerate until needed.

ENTRÉE Beef Filet Mignon with Mustard and Herb Crust (page 128).

Hot Tip Coat the beef in the mustard mixture earlier in the day, and refrigerate. Take it out of the fridge 30 minutes before you're ready to cook it, and season with salt and pepper just before cooking.

SIDE Herb and Garlic Roasted New Potatoes (page 154).

Hot Tip Earlier in the day, get the potatoes in the baking dish, covered and ready to cook according to the recipe. Also, chop the herbs ahead of time.

DESSERT Chocolate Fondue with Seasonal Fruits (page 197).

Brunch for Four or Six

In addition to considering the seating availability in your apartment, this petite ensemble requires a little forethought, as what you prepare will be dictated by how many guests you invite and how many hangovers you have been assigned to cure. If you know you'll receive a desperate call from one of your guests claiming she's "experiencing the worst hangover of my life," then you might want to consider a brunch centered on crispy bacon and Bloody Marys. If your crew is feeling the pressure to impress the single boys at your college roommate's wedding next weekend, then perhaps a lighter menu will suit their fancy.

celebration (or for no reason at all!) champagne brunch menu suggestions

COCKTAIL Peach-Infused Prosecco (Italian sparkling wine): Per drink, combine ¾ cup Prosecco with ¼ cup Hansen's Diet Peach soda

SALAD Grilled Radicchio and Arugula Salad with Lemon Vinaigrette (page 55), recipe times four

Hot Tip Make vinaigrette the day before. Grill arugula earlier in the day, cover, and refrigerate. Assemble salad just before you're ready to serve it.

ENTRÉE Spinach, Bacon, and Fontina Frittata (page 143), recipe times two

Hot Tip Make earlier in the morning. Serve at room temperature, or re-warm in the oven at 350°F until it's heated through. (Do this as guests arrive, and once it's hot, lower the temperature to 200°F to keep it warm. Make sure to cover it to prevent it from drying out.)

DESSERT Baked Peaches Stuffed with Amaretti Cookies (page 194), recipe times four

Hot Tip Make the day before and reheat in the oven at 350°F or serve at room temperature.

studio or small apartment continued

Cocktail Party for Six or Eight

No longer do two medium pizzas and a case of Natty Light constitute a cocktail party. Pony up, ladies; it's time to up the ante. If your studio is a single room large enough for only your bed and a couch, consider hosting a fuss-free cocktail party with your nearest and dearest troops. Keep in mind that you might not have enough seating for everyone. Consider purchasing a few large throw pillows to introduce alternative floor seating, thus creating a more intimate space for conversing. Utilize your kitchen as the staging area, chock-full of cocktails and simple hors d'oeuvres. By creating an epicenter of fun, whether it's a studio or tiny one-bedroom, you'll avoid having to clean up a sticky mess throughout your entire apartment. That's not to say that you shouldn't have a couple of smaller plates with appetizers placed in the middle of your gaggle of pals—on your coffee table or dresser top. Depending on how large your space is and how many throw pillows you bought, you can easily support a cocktail party that your neighbors will complain about.

uptown cocktail party for eight

Count on each guest having three of each hors d'oeuvre. That's more than most will eat, but that will make up for the former frat guy who eats six of everything.

COCKTAIL Vodka Martini: In a cocktail shaker, combine ice with 2 parts vodka, 1 part vermouth. Strain into a chilled martini glass. Float a lemon slice in each glass and garnish with a green olive on a pick.

HORS D'OEUVRE UNE Classic Caprese Bruschetta. Use the recipe for Classic Caprese (page 52), recipe times four

Hot Tip Slice and toast a baguette earlier in the day, then just before serving top with a slice of tomato, salt, pepper, cheese, basil, and good extra-virgin olive oil.

HORS D'OEUVRE DEUX Bruschetta with Basil Pesto (page 231) and Beef Filet Mignon with Mustard and Herb Crust (page 128), both recipes times three

Hot Tip Make basil pesto up to a week ahead, and store in the freezer. Earlier in the day, cook beef, cover, and store in the fridge. Slice and toast baguettes. Bring beef to room temperature and slice just before serving; cut into bite-sized pieces so you'll end up with at least 24 pieces. To serve, spread pesto on toasts and top with a slice of beef.

HORS D'OEUVRE TROIS Scampi-Style Shrimp (page 138), recipe times four

Hot Tip Make earlier in the day. Serve chilled or at room temperature with toothpicks.

HORS D'OEUVRE QUATRE Grilled Pineapple with Vanilla-Coconut Ricotta (page 200), recipe times three

Hot Tip Cut each ring of pineapple into fourths, so each recipe will serve four people. Earlier in the day, grill pineapple and make ricotta mixture. Cover both and keep in the fridge. Also, toast coconut. Assemble prior to serving.

apartment or house (shared or solo)

If you live in an apartment with a separate kitchen, bathroom, bedroom, living room, and/or dining room, then chances are you'll be inclined to host events that include a larger invite list. The following menu suggestions utilize your location's fullest potential. Also, while your guest lists may ebb and flow, the menu suggestions for the events mentioned for studios and small apartments can be used in your larger apartment as well.

Patio Barbecue for Eight or Ten

You've never balked at a challenge and you're not about to give in to one now. Barbecues have typically been deemed a man's domain. We beg to differ. Despite your aversion to using a grill and your inability to light a fire with anything less than an entire bottle of lighter fluid, you are absolutely capable of preparing an outrageously fantastic smorgasbord of barbecue goodies. Impress your friends and boyfriend, or soon-to-be-boyfriend once he witnesses the ease with which you handle meat, with the following recipes. Soon your friends will be hounding you to help strategize about menu selections for their next shindig.

backyard barbecue bonanza for ten

Multiply each recipe by ten for this soiree.

COCKTAIL Mojito: For each drink, fill a glass with 10 to 15 mint leaves and crush using a wooden spoon. Add ice and 1 packet of Splenda, and pour in 2 ounces water, 1 ounce lime juice, and 1 ounce rum. Garnish the side of the glass with a wedge of lime and a sprig of mint leaves.

ENTRÉE Classic American Burger (page 129), one per guest

Hot Tip Offer an array of cheeses and condiments for your guests so they can build their perfect burger.

SIDE Grilled Asparagus with Fresh Lemon and Olives (page 76), recipe times ten (two bundles of asparagus)

Hot Tip Trim and clean asparagus earlier in the day. Also, chop the olives.

SIDE Roasted New Potato Salad with (page 155), recipe times ten

Hot Tip Make vinaigrette the day before and store in the fridge. Earlier in the day cook the corn, slice the red peppers, and chop the olives.

DESSERT Baked Stuffed Banana with Graham Cracker Spoons (page 195), one per guest

Hot Tip Earlier in the day, assemble bananas, wrap in foil, and refrigerate. Cook them in a covered grill until soft.

apartment or house (shared or solo) continued

April Showers Bring May Flowers (And June Brings Weddings to Attend and Babies to Be Born)

Yes, showers can be painful. Yes, you think you might poke yourself in the eye with a pencil if you are forced to participate in another perfunctory bridal or baby shower quiz. No, you do not *know* the groom's favorite color, meal, or sports team. Nor do you care to *ever* know. There, we've said it. Unnerving as that may be, we're confident you'll throw at least a shower or two. Once the wedding showers wane, the baby showers will surface. Until you're thrown the hot potato, we'd recommend the following menus for throwing delightful showers for those who currently reside on the marital or mommy throne. (These menus are perfect as buffet-style or formal sit-down lunches.)

shower for eight or ten

Serve this buffet-style so you can spend more time with your guests than in the kitchen fussing.

COCKTAIL Raspberry Lemonade: Per two drinks, in a cocktail shaker combine ice with 2 cups unsweetened lemonade iced tea, 1 pack Splenda, and 2 ounces vodka. Garnish with fresh raspberries floating in each glass.

ENTRÉE UNE Curried Scallops (page 130), recipe times five

Hot Tip Make a batch just before guests arrive, then replenish it as necessary. Serve warm with toothpicks.

ENTRÉE DEUX Caramelized Onion Frittata with Parmesan and Balsamic Glaze (page 142), recipe times two

Hot Tip Make earlier in the day, then reheat in the oven at 350°F or serve at room temperature. Cut into bite-sized pieces.

ENTRÉE TROIS Pizza with Shaved Fennel, Shallots, Green Olives, and Mozzarella (page 188), recipe times three. Cut each pizza into fourths.

Hot Tip Earlier in the day shave the fennel, slice the shallots, and chop the olives. If your pizza dough is already stored in the freezer, bring to room temperature prior to using.

ENTRÉE QUATRE Easiest-Ever Mixed Greens Salad with Lemon Vinaigrette (page 47), recipe times ten

Hot Tip Make vinaigrette the day before and store in the fridge.

DESSERT Plum and Peach Shortcake with Cinnamon Cream (page 201), recipe times ten.

Hot Tip Make cinnamon cream the day before and refrigerate, covered. Make the fruit mixture earlier in the day and keep in the fridge until ready to serve.

apartment or house (shared or solo) continued

The TV Dinner That Doesn't Involve a Microwave

Whether you claim to be averse to television or have been a self-proclaimed junkie since *Kids Incorporated* and *Punky Brewster*, chances are you'll host an evening when your TV is the impetus for your entertainment. Perhaps you discovered that the animal channel is previewing a special on endangered tortoise pro-creation methods, and you'll be apt to invite a few friends over to watch. Or your latest HBO addiction is having its season finale, and you'll plan an evening to commemorate the occasion. The simplicity of the following menu recommendations will prevent you from ever being tempted to offer your friends a mea-sly frozen pizza and a rancid glass of red wine (from the jug that's been open for two weeks) ever again. Perhaps they'll be so impressed they'll return the favor and invite you over to their place for the next season finale.

tv viewing party for four or six

BEVERAGE Root Beer Floats (These aren't your Grandmother's root beer floats.) Mix 1 cup diet root beer with 1 ounce vanilla vodka, and pour over ice. (Makes one serving.)

SALAD Spinach and Roasted Peppers with Balsamic-Herb Vinaigrette (page 57), recipe times six

Hot Tip Make vinaigrette the day before and store in the fridge.

ENTRÉE Fusilli with Turkey Italian Sausage, Green Peas, and Mozzarella (page 170), recipe times six

DESSERT Caramel Apple Strudel (page 196), recipe times three

Hot Tip This can be baked the day before, stored in the fridge, and reheated in the oven at 350°F when you need it.

Attention to Detail:
Accessorizing Your Events

The following items and ideas will elevate your gatherings from apathetic beer blowouts to savvy and sophisticated soirees. Attention to detail is critical to fostering the perfect environment for each of your events, from an intimate dinner party of four to a cocktail party of six, from a bridal shower of ten to a backyard barbecue on a Sunday afternoon.

Plates (Paper and Everyday): Whether you're serving with your Grandmother's 1956 everyday ware or you've purchased a brand new set from Crate & Barrel, always remember that your dishes are the foundation for your event. Get creative. Mix and match. Most of all, enjoy! Just remember, make sure you have enough to serve your friends.

Glassware (Plastic and Everyday): All we ask is that you have enough for your guests to drink with.

Silverware (Plastic and Everyday): Again, we beg that you have enough for your guests to eat with. If you're serving dessert separate from the meal, be sure you have enough for each guest to have a fresh utensil. So fresh and so clean.

Serving Bowls and Platters: The more the merrier, in our estimation.

Napkins (Cocktail and Dinner): Napkins are an inexpensive way to increase the detail of your event. You never know when you'll throw your next cocktail or dinner party. Therefore, always keep a spectrum of cocktail and dinner napkins handy. More often than not, napkins are available in fabulous designs and colors that will accentuate your plates, glassware, and table settings.

Candles: Leveraging candlelight will increase the intimacy of your event and many times will complement the setting in a more beneficial way than loud and bright overhead lighting. Always keep a variety of candles on hand: tea candles, tall hurricanes, and floating candles. There are a handful of scented candles that are spectacular. Be wary, however, as there are many that will overpower your apartment. Consequently, your friends might become overwhelmed by the smell and won't be able to enjoy your delicious spread.

Flowers: *Fresh*. Always *fresh*. You can never go wrong with flowers. They are the ultimate accessory to a woman and any event she hosts.

Vases: For your flowers, of course.

Food stationing: A kitchen table, island, or kitchen counters are the best place to station your buffet as it contains your mess in one location. If, however, you have a dining room, and you're not sitting around the table, stationing a beautiful spread around the table is always a wonderful option. Simply remove the chairs and place them in the living room for seating. Display your entrees around the dining room table. Remember, adding layers to your table, such as flowers, vases, or hurricane candles, offers a little eye candy to your arrangement. Don't forget that utensils, plates, and napkins also add color and texture to your table.

appendix a
the little black apron sample menus

We all know that the "little black dress" exists to be accessorized and thus transformed to fit any occasion out on the town. Here are a few of our suggestions on how to mix and match your recipes, creating an endless repertoire to fit any given occasion in your dining room. The following recipes have been paired because of their complementing flavors. In addition, many of the recipes have similar ingredients and, therefore, you'll find preparation a wee bit easier (and cheaper), given their commonalities. We're always searching for creative combinations with our wardrobes, so why stop there? Confidence and creativity are in many ways joined at the hip. The recipes that follow should be considered foundations for your culinary canvas. Mix and match, create your own, and live on the edge. Consider it *The Little Black Apron* kitchen paint-by-numbers.

appendix b
quick reference guide to vinaigrettes, sauces, and marinades

Vinaigrettes
PAGES 227–29

Vinaigrettes can be stored in your refrigerator for 3 to 5 days, so make enough to use it a few times. Leftover vinaigrettes are also great as quick sauces, dressing, and marinades for chicken, pork, beef, and seafood.

Sauces and Marinades
PAGES 229–35

All of these sauces can be made in bulk and stored in the freezer for quick meal options. Store them in ice cube trays and pop out one cube per serving.

Balsamic-Herb Vinaigrette

MAKES ABOUT ¼ CUP, ENOUGH FOR 2 TO 3 SERVINGS

1 tablespoon balsamic vinegar

1 small clove garlic, finely chopped (or use a garlic press), about ¼ teaspoon

½ teaspoon Dijon mustard

½ teaspoon finely chopped fresh rosemary (leaves only, no stems)

½ teaspoon finely chopped fresh thyme (leaves only, no stems)

2 teaspoons finely chopped Italian parsley

2 tablespoons extra-virgin olive oil

Salt and pepper to taste

Put all the ingredients in a bowl and whisk vigorously until they're well combined.

Blue Cheese Vinaigrette

MAKES ABOUT ¼ CUP, ENOUGH FOR 2 TO 3 SERVINGS

1 ounce crumbled blue cheese

1 tablespoon champagne vinegar

2 tablespoons extra-virgin olive oil

½ tablespoon chopped fresh Italian flat-leaf parsley

Salt and pepper to taste

1. Combine the first three ingredients in a blender or food processor, and process until smooth, about 5 to 7 seconds.

2. Stir in the parsley, salt, and pepper.

Champagne Vinaigrette

MAKES ABOUT ¼ CUP, ENOUGH FOR 2 TO 3 SERVINGS

1 tablespoon champagne vinegar

2 tablespoons extra-virgin olive oil

Salt and pepper to taste

Put all the ingredients in a bowl and whisk vigorously until they're well combined.

Cilantro Vinaigrette

MAKES ABOUT ⅓ CUP, ENOUGH FOR 3 TO 4 SERVINGS

½ bunch fresh cilantro, with bottom inch or so of the stems removed

1 tablespoon red wine vinegar

½ tablespoon lime juice, from about half a lime

1 clove garlic, minced (or use a garlic press)

½ tablespoon chopped red onion

¼ teaspoon ground cumin

¼ teaspoon ground ancho chili powder (can be found in the spice aisle of most supermarkets)

3 tablespoons light extra-virgin olive oil

Salt and pepper to taste

Put all the ingredients in a bowl and whisk vigorously until they're combined.

Citrus Vinaigrette

MAKES ABOUT ¼ CUP, ENOUGH FOR 2 TO 3 SERVINGS

1 teaspoon fresh lemon juice

1 teaspoon fresh orange juice

1 teaspoon fresh lime juice

2 tablespoons extra-virgin olive oil

Salt and pepper to taste

Put all the ingredients in a bowl and whisk vigorously until they're well combined.

Grapefruit Vinaigrette

MAKES ABOUT ¼ CUP, ENOUGH FOR 2 TO 3 SERVINGS

1 tablespoon fresh grapefruit juice

2 tablespoons extra-virgin olive oil

Salt and pepper to taste

Put all the ingredients in a bowl and whisk vigorously until they're well combined.

Lemon Vinaigrette

MAKES ABOUT ¼ CUP, ENOUGH FOR 2 TO 3 SERVINGS

1 tablespoon fresh lemon juice

2 tablespoons extra-virgin olive oil

Salt and pepper to taste

Put all the ingredients in a bowl and whisk vigorously until they're well combined.

Sesame Garlic Vinaigrette

MAKES ABOUT ¼ CUP, ENOUGH FOR 2 TO 3 SERVINGS

1 tablespoon rice vinegar

2 tablespoons extra-virgin olive oil, extra-light flavor

¼ teaspoon sesame oil

1 small clove garlic, minced (or use a garlic press)

1 teaspoon light soy sauce

Put all the ingredients in a bowl and whisk vigorously until they're well combined.

Sesame Vinaigrette

MAKES ABOUT ¼ CUP, ENOUGH FOR 2 TO 3 SERVINGS

1½ tablespoons rice wine vinegar

1½ tablespoons sugar or sugar substitute (Splenda)

¼ teaspoon sesame oil

1 teaspoon chopped fresh cilantro (leaves only, no stems)

Salt and pepper to taste

Put all the ingredients in a bowl and whisk vigorously until they're well combined.

Whole-Grain Mustard Dressing

MAKES ABOUT ¼ CUP, ENOUGH FOR 2 TO 3 SERVINGS

1 tablespoon lemon juice

2 tablespoons extra-virgin olive oil

2 teaspoons whole-grain mustard

1 tablespoon finely chopped shallot

1 small garlic clove, finely chopped (or use a garlic press)

Salt and pepper to taste

Put all the ingredients in a bowl and whisk vigorously until they're well combined.

Almond-Olive Relish

MAKES ABOUT ¼ CUP

Use with chicken, pork, or seafood.

1 teaspoon extra-virgin olive oil

1 shallot, thinly sliced

1 tablespoon chopped picholine (or other green) olives

1 tablespoon chopped roasted red bell pepper

1½ tablespoons coarsely chopped toasted almonds

1 teaspoon chopped Italian flat-leaf parsley

Salt and pepper to taste

1. Heat a skillet over medium low heat, add the shallots, and cook until the shallots are translucent. Remove the shallots and place in a bowl.

2. Add the olives, peppers, almonds, and parsley and stir to combine.

3. Season the relish with salt and pepper.

Balsamic Glaze

MAKES 2 TABLESPOONS

Use on chicken, pork, seafood, and grilled veggies.

¼ cup (4 tablespoons) balsamic vinegar

Pour the vinegar into a small saucepan. Bring it to a boil over high heat and reduce it by half. Keep your eye on it because it will reduce quickly.

Basic Tomato Sauce

MAKES ABOUT 2 CUPS

1 tablespoon extra-virgin olive oil

½ small onion, diced

2 cloves garlic, minced (or use a garlic press)

¼ bunch roughly chopped fresh basil (leaves only, no stems), about ⅓ to ½ cup

1 (14-ounce) can crushed tomatoes

Salt and pepper to taste

1. Heat a saucepan over medium heat and add the olive oil. When the pan is hot, add the onions and cook about 4 minutes, or until the onions are soft and translucent but not browned.

2. Add the garlic and cook 1 minute. Add the basil and tomatoes. Bring to a boil, then reduce the heat to low, cover, and simmer 15 to 30 minutes, stirring occasionally.

3. Season with salt and pepper. If the sauce gets too thick, just add a little water or low-sodium chicken broth.

Basil Pesto

MAKES ABOUT ⅓ CUP

Use on chicken, pork, beef, seafood, and veggies,

1 cup fresh basil leaves, packed

1 tablespoon pine nuts, toasted

2 tablespoons grated Parmesan cheese

1 clove garlic, chopped (or use a garlic press)

2 tablespoons extra-virgin olive oil

2 tablespoons water

Juice of half a lemon

Salt and pepper to taste

Combine all the ingredients in a food processor or blender and blend until they're smooth. If you're using a blender, you may need to add a little more oil or water so that it can blend.

Coconut Curry

MAKES ABOUT 2 CUPS

Use on chicken, pork, beef, seafood, and veggies.

2 shallots, thinly sliced

2 teaspoons curry powder

1 can light coconut milk

Juice of 1 lime

2 teaspoons chopped fresh cilantro (leaves only, no stems)

2 tablespoons chopped fresh basil (leaves only, no stems)

Salt and pepper to taste

1. Heat a skillet over medium high heat and coat it with the olive oil.

2. Add the shallots and cook until the shallots are translucent.

3. Add the curry powder and cook for 30 seconds.

4. Add the coconut milk and simmer on low heat for 7 to 8 minutes.

5. Add and stir the lime juice, cilantro, and basil and season with salt and pepper.

Enchilada Sauce

MAKES ABOUT 1½ CUPS

½ small onion, sliced thin

1 tablespoon ancho chili powder

1 teaspoon cumin

1 16-ounce can crushed tomatoes

Salt and pepper to taste

Makes about ½ cup

1. Heat a 1-quart pot over medium heat and coat it with the olive oil.

2. Add the onion, ancho chili powder, and cumin and stir together using a wooden spoon or heat-resistant spatula. Cook for 5 to 8 minutes, until the onions are translucent.

3. Add the tomatoes and bring to a boil.

4. Turn down the heat and let it simmer for 15 minutes, stirring occasionally.

5. Season with salt and pepper.

Ginger-Soy Marinade

MAKES ABOUT ¼ CUP

Use on chicken, pork, beef, and seafood.

2 tablespoons soy sauce

1 teaspoon fresh ginger, peeled and minced (or grated with a microplane)

Juice of half a lime

1 small clove garlic, minced (or use a garlic press)

1 scallion or green onion, finely chopped

Combine all the ingredients well with a spoon.

Hoisin Glaze

MAKES ABOUT ½ CUP

Use on chicken, pork, beef, and seafood.

¼ cup hoisin sauce

2 cloves garlic, chopped (or use a garlic press)

1" piece of fresh ginger, peeled and chopped (or grated with a microplane)

2 tablespoons low-sodium soy sauce

Put all the ingredients in a bowl and whisk vigorously until they're well combined.

Latin American Chimichurri Sauce

MAKES ABOUT ½ CUP

Use on chicken, pork, beef, and seafood.

1 clove garlic, chopped (or use a garlic press)

¼ bunch fresh Italian flat-leaf parsley, tough stems removed

¼ bunch fresh cilantro, tough stems removed

Juice of half a lime

½ tablespoon red wine vinegar

2 tablespoons extra-virgin olive oil

½ jalapeño, seeded (optional)

Salt and pepper to taste

Put all the ingredients into a food processor or blender and blend until they're well combined. The sauce should be still slightly chunky.

Miso Glaze

MAKES ABOUT ¼ CUP

Use on chicken, pork, beef, and seafood.

½ tablespoon sweet white miso (found in the Asian foods aisle or specialty refrigerated section of your supermarket)

½ tablespoon mirin (sweet Japanese cooking wine found in the Asian foods aisle)

½ tablespoon rice wine vinegar

½ tablespoon honey

1 teaspoon soy sauce

1 small clove garlic, minced (or use a garlic press)

½ teaspoon fresh ginger, peeled and minced (or grated with a microplane)

Salt and pepper to taste

Put all the ingredients in a bowl and whisk vigorously until they're well combined.

Miso Marinade*

MAKES ABOUT ¼ CUP

Use on chicken, pork, beef, and seafood.

1 tablespoon sweet white miso

2 tablespoons mirin wine

½ tablespoon honey

1 teaspoon soy sauce

1 small clove garlic, minced (or use a garlic press)

½ teaspoon fresh ginger, peeled and minced (or grated with a microplane)

Put all the ingredients in a bowl and whisk vigorously until they're well combined.

*A glaze has a thick syrupy consistency, whereas a marinade, depending on what it's made of, can be completely watery.

Pepperonata

MAKES ABOUT ½ CUP

Use on chicken, pork, beef, and seafood.

½ tablespoon extra-virgin olive oil

½ small red bell pepper, seeded and cut into ¼" strips

1 teaspoon balsamic vinegar

1 clove garlic, minced (or use a garlic press)

½ tablespoon pitted and chopped kalamata olives

½ tablespoon capers, drained

Salt and pepper to taste

1 teaspoon chopped fresh basil (leaves only, no stems)

1. Heat a 7" sauté pan over medium low heat and coat it with ½ tablespoon of olive oil.

2. Add the bell peppers and cook until the peppers are very soft (but not browned), about 15 minutes.

3. Add the balsamic vinegar and the garlic and cook until fragrant, about 30 seconds.

4. Stir in the olives, capers, salt, pepper, and basil. Remove the pan from the heat.

Romesco Sauce

MAKES ABOUT ½ CUP

Use on chicken, pork, beef, and seafood.

1 clove garlic, chopped (or use a garlic press)

1 roasted red bell pepper

¼ cup toasted almonds

Juice of half a lemon

1 tablespoon extra-virgin olive oil

Salt and pepper to taste

Combine all the ingredients in a food processor or blender and blend until they're smooth.

Sun-Dried Tomato Pesto

MAKES ABOUT ½ CUP

Use on chicken, pork, beef, and seafood.

½ cup sun-dried tomatoes packed in olive oil, drained well

1 tablespoon toasted almonds

1 small clove garlic, chopped (or use a garlic press)

2 tablespoons grated Parmesan cheese

1 teaspoon fresh lemon juice (juice of about half a lemon)

Salt and pepper to taste

Combine all the ingredients in a food processor or blender. Blend until smooth, about 15 to 20 seconds.

Tomato-Basil Salsa

MAKES ABOUT ½ CUP

Use on chicken, pork, beef, and especially seafood.

1 small tomato, diced

1 tablespoon chopped fresh basil leaves

½ small clove garlic, minced (or use a garlic press)

1 teaspoon good extra-virgin olive oil

Salt and pepper to taste

Combine all the ingredients well with a spoon.

basic measurements and conversions

Volume

3 teaspoons	1 tablespoon
2 tablespoons	1 ounce
8 ounces	1 cup
1 teaspoon	5 ml
1 tablespoon	15 ml
¼ cup	60 ml
⅓ cup	80 ml
½ cup	120 ml
1 cup	240 ml
1 pint *(2 cups)*	470 ml
1 quart *(4 cups)*	.95 liters
1 gallon *(16 cups)*	3.8 liters

Weight

1 ounce	28 grams
1 pound *(16 ounces)*	454 grams

Length

1 inch	2.54 cm
1 foot *(12 inches)*	30.48 cm

index of recipes

index of topics

about the authors

© Elaine Mayes

MELISSA (left), JODI (center), and KATIE constitute a mini–United Nations within a nation—the Hawaiian WASP, the Long Island Jew, and the Southern California Mexican. Although the ease with which the term *diversity* is uttered in these politically correct times is a bit unnerving, we do think it's worth mentioning for this reason: four generations ago our great-great-grandparents were speaking three different languages in three different countries: Spanish in Mexico, Yiddish in Poland, and Hawaiian in Hawaii. It was our mothers' and grandmothers' kitchens—however ethnically and geographically separated—that brought us together. Our appreciation for the warmth of a kitchen, the love of cooking, and our families transcends culture, age, and language and embraces a universal appreciation of wellness. It is this heritage that motivated each of us to pursue culinary exploration: Melissa as a writer, Jodi as a nutritionist, and Katie as a chef.

Melissa Gibson

Melissa was born and raised in Honolulu, Hawaii, and is seventh generation to the islands. Much like her ancestors, Melissa has spent a great deal of time traveling and accumulating adventure stories, which are at her disposal during dull cocktail parties. After receiving her undergraduate degree in public policy from Duke University, she moved to San Francisco to work in marketing for a variety of *Fortune* 500 companies. She has also lived in Paris, France, where she studied French language and art history, and Barra de Navidad, Mexico, where she worked on location for a Fox Searchlight film. Her willingness to break out her pocketbook and dive deeper into the red is a direct result of her love for cultures and exploration. From Rio de Janeiro to

Edinburgh to Florence to Hong Kong to Madrid to Milwaukee, Melissa is constantly amazed by food's ability to traverse race, culture, class, and language, no matter where she is in the world. She currently lives in San Francisco, California.

Jodi Citrin, M.S., R.D.

Jodi Citrin is a registered dietitian and president of Citrition, LLC, a nutrition counseling practice in New York City that attracts clients from across the country including models, news anchors, and celebrities. In addition to private counseling, Jodi is often asked to speak at corporations, nonprofit organizations, hospitals, and universities throughout New York and New Jersey. Jodi is also the national spokesperson for Dannon Danimals yogurt. She has appeared on *Good Morning America* and radio stations such as Radio Disney and CNN International, as well as in publications such as *Fitness*, *Parenting*, and *Kiwi* magazines.

Jodi graduated cum laude from Duke University with a degree in biology, received her master's degree in nutrition and dietetics from New York University, and completed an internship at Mt. Sinai Hospital. She is a member of the American Dietetic Association, Nutrition Entrepreneurs, and the Greater New York Dietetic Association.

Katie Nuanes

Growing up in Southern California with its spectrum of ethnicities, Katie learned to love the breadth of cultural cuisine. Her curiosity continued to grow during her travels throughout Europe, Central and South America, the Caribbean, and Northern Africa and played a significant role in developing her love of all types of food and her respect for the authentic integrity of each culture. While attending UCLA, Katie turned her love of food and cooking into a career-driven passion and knew culinary school was the place for her. At the California School of Culinary Arts in Pasadena, Katie studied classic French fundamentals with modern applications, as well as applied business in the food service industry and menu planning. She won academic awards for excellence and graduated with honors. After working at the highly acclaimed Greens Restaurant in San Francisco, her quest for creative license drove her to become a personal chef in Orange County, California, where she currently resides.